No, Really, Where Are **You** From?

Personal Stories of Chinese Identity Retention and Loss

Second Edition

Nancy Ng

No, Really, Where Are You From? Personal Stories of Chinese Identity Retention and Loss

Copyright © 2012 by Nancy Ng

All rights reserved. No part of this book may be reproduced or transmitted in any form or by any means without written permission of the author.

ISBN 978-1479231379

Publisher: Nancy Ng (Edmonton, Alberta, Canada)

Book Cover design: Jessica Hopley

Printer: Kindle Direct Publishing

Editor: Norma Jean (NJ) Brown

Proofreader: Vivian Giang/Wei Wong

Contact information:

Facebook page: Nancy's Library

Dedico este libro a mi abuelo, Julio Ng, y a mi padre, Santiago Ng.

TABLE OF CONTENTS

Acknowledgement 7

About The Author 8

Foreword 9

From Then To Now 15

Señorita Maracay 25

A Soup Called Love 47

Chinese Men Can Jump! 57

And The Tony Award Goes To... Marty Chan 85

Cheez Whiz Over Steamed Rice, Please! 102

The Sky's The Limit 120

Gardens of Hope 133

Finding Michelle 144

We Are Family 172

Final Remarks 186

Bibliography 193

Appendix 196

Acknowledgement

Throughout the 7 years it took to put this book together, I have received a tremendous amount of support from people who have contributed to this book by inspiring me, giving advice, providing leads, or lending me emotional support.

Santiago Ng: Muchas gracias y te quiero, papi.

Julia Chen and Maxwell Chen: You will forever be my Princess (Boo) and Bumblebee (Bee). You are the sunshine of my life ... a BIG kiss and BIG hug!

Susan P.: I know I can always count on you for your continuing support, encouragement, and advice. You have helped me more than you will ever know.

Rick and Dianne Westwood: Thank you for your help and support. I will never forget it.

About The Author

This is Nancy Ng's first book. In 2005, she began work on No, Really, Where Are You From? because she was tired of having to explain why a Chinese looking girl ended up being born in Venezuela and has a Canadian accent. Besides being detained by immigration officers while abroad because "nothing in her passport matches" (imagine having your birthplace listed as Venezuela and citizenship as Canadian, while looking Chinese!), Nancy has also been "explaining" this different background for most of her life. And she's tired of it. The constant curiosity from others of her cultural backgrounds eventually lead to writing this book. She knows cultural identity is a sensitive topic that can be up there with religion or even politics, but we need to talk about it. She also wanted to write this book because she often wonders what would have become of her, if she had never left Venezuela and grew up Venezuelan. Rather than returning to Venezuela and interviewing Chinese individuals born and raised there, Nancy looked closer to home for answers. Through her graduate work, she was able to further explore cultural identity and eventually her Chinese identity with No, Really, Where Are You From?

Nancy has also written and produced a play, The Yellow Peril, for the 2003 Edmonton Fringe Festival. She graduated from the University of Alberta (Edmonton, Alberta, Canada) with a BA in Sociology, and graduated from Carleton University (Ottawa, Ontario, Canada) with an MA in Sociology. She lives in Edmonton, Alberta, Canada. The theme of her second book will be on resiliency and perseverance, and her third book will be about our fears of death and the funeral world.

Foreword

Although I was born in Venezuela, and immigrated to Canada when I was seven years old, I am of Chinese descent. It took me a long time to arrive at the point in my life where I had any interest in my Chinese background, but when I finally got to that point, my interest in the subject went far beyond idle curiosity. I delved into the subject to the degree that the topic of my final essay for my Master's Degree in Sociology was a comparison between ethnic identity retention in early Chinese immigrants in the late 1800s and current Chinese immigrants from Hong Kong.

By the time I was finished exploring that topic, I had began to think, seriously, for the first time in my life, about how my own cultural background had affected the person I had become. And I wondered how other people in similar circumstances were impacted by their experiences. I wanted to know what the common struggles were and how people responded to them. But I was tired of analyzing statistics, dissecting graphs, and reading other academics' analyses on the topic. I was also becoming increasingly uncomfortable with academic versions and analyses of the stories—somewhere, I thought, between the mouths of the real people to the ears of academia, something is bound to be misunderstood or misinterpreted. I wanted to hear the stories of the people who had actually lived these experiences. And so I went on a search for a book that might answer some of the questions I had. But there was none to be found.

And then, one day, while I was watching Oprah, she introduced her guest, Po Bronson. I had no idea at that point who he was or what he was all about (beyond the fact that he was very attractive, which, admittedly, is probably the main reason I kept watching). It turned out that the subject of the interview was a book he had written called What Should I do with my Life? The book consists of a series of interviews with people from all walks of life. In the book, Bronson tells the stories of these people—their lives, their careers, and, most importantly, how they dared to be honest with themselves. By the time the interview was over, I knew I had to read this book. I bought myself a copy, took it with me on a trip to Africa, and read it between safaris and museum visits. Suddenly, the vague notion of writing a book, which had been an idea floating around in my head for a while, came into focus. And I knew that I would take Bronson's lead and write a book told through the voices of the people who had lived the experiences I was trying to capture.

But I still had no clear cut plan. I knew that I wanted to explore the issue of Chinese people and their cultural identities, but initially—undoubtedly because of my connections to Venezuela—I thought that I would focus on Chinese people who were born and raised in the most "unlikely" places in the world, such as Africa or South America. I wanted to explore environments where the culture of the country was more homogenous and not as diverse as it is in, for instance, North America or Europe. I soon realized, however, that this might present a challenge that I would be unable to overcome, given how expensive it would be and the limitations of my Spanish and Chinese. And then it occurred to me: why not interview Chinese people who were born and raised in the most unlikely places in Canada -- small towns? It didn't make any sense to interview Chinese individuals born and raised in a large cosmopolitan city because of their easy access to their cultural resources. Eventually I added to this a second group: Chinese people who were born in the 1930s, 40s, or 50s in either Edmonton or Calgary. I chose these two cities for two reasons—one being convenience and the other being that, during the years in question, both cities had a very low (or non existent) Chinese population. I found this method was the closest I could simulate an environment (the small town simulating a homogenous Venezuela) parallel to what I, as a visible minority, would have grown up in if I had stayed in Venezuela. The bottom line was that I wanted to know how these people negotiated their status as members of a visible minority in such a "white" environment. I looked at how issues such as family size, the presence of extended family, occupation, education, and a variety of other factors came into play. (For a list of the specific questions I used to guide the interviews, see the Appendix.)

I want to make an important distinction between urban mainstream occupations versus rural mainstream occupations, which will be mentioned throughout the book. The key concept in such a distinction is the intensity of the interaction with the mainstream population. In this book, urban mainstream occupations refer to professional careers that would allow the Chinese person to interact more with mainstream society. Professions in this category would include physicians, engineers, lawyers, or dentists. Non mainstream occupations in urban areas have less interaction with mainstream society, but more with the Chinese community. A few examples include working in a laundromat, or as a waiter/waitress for a Chinese restaurant. In these occupations, the Chinese immigrants may not speak much English, have little money and education, and work with others of similar cultural backgrounds. Thus, they rely on and help each other in the new land. This, like the early Chinese immigrants' experiences, helps sustain the Chinese culture.

In the rural setting, a different dynamic occurs. The Chinese family owned restaurants, the Chinese factory worker, the Chinese physician, the Chinese dentist, or the Chinese potato farmer would be rural mainstream occupations because of their increased interaction with the mainstream population. In the rural setting, there wouldn't be any non-mainstream occupations because the majority of the population in these areas are Caucasian, and there would be less cultural resources for the Chinese to access along with a smaller Chinese population to interact with.

But I didn't want to analyze them sociologically—I just wanted to hear their stories, and let the stories themselves lead the discussion.

Of course the question still remained of how I would find these people. With a little bit of creativity, and a lot of persistence, I found my interviewees in a variety of ways. Kevin Kwan, Marty Chan and Wei Wong are people I already knew. I found Michelle Wong through a local travel magazine. Mary Chan and Susan P. both work with me. I contacted former Lt. Governor Kwong via his secretaries, and I found Wayne Leong through his father's obituary, which I read in the paper one Saturday morning. These eight people were, I thought, the ones who were "meant" to be included in my book—they are a diverse group in terms of age, gender, sexual orientation, education, and occupation. And most importantly, they were willing to talk to me about their experiences—not all that easy to come by within the Chinese population.

When I began interviewing people, I was astonished by their openness and their candour. And in response to that, I found myself becoming more open as well. It was, in fact, the courage of the interviewees that gave me the courage to tell my own story (not to mention the realization that, if I expected other people to tell their stories, I had better be willing to tell my own!). This is not to say that I still wasn't nervous putting my life down on paper—in fact, because I'm normally a very private person, I felt like I might be attempting to walk on broken glass barefoot. I worried constantly about what I was going to write, and what people, especially other Chinese people, would say when they read it. Would they want to crucify me? Burn me at the stake? Gut wrenching dread would be the closest description to what I felt. But when the proverbial mighty pen touched the vulnerable paper, there was no turning back, and at some point I just stopped worrying about what other people might think. I soon had over 20 pages of feelings, facts, and reflections. And I knew at that point that I had become a more honest person—that I had learned to stay true to myself because of the honesty of the eight people I interviewed.

The degree to which the people in this book, myself included, struggled with their Chinese identity varies, as does the degree to which they were influenced by the Chinese culture. There were no black and white answers to the questions I had—the answers were neither predictable nor consistent. These are truly individual experiences. While it might seem reasonable to expect to see a linear evolution in people's perceptions of being Chinese as they move from childhood to adulthood, those perceptions are subject to change at any given time, even as people enter their senior years. There are so many factors involved in shaping a person that cultural identity (or even identity itself) is not a concept that can be easily pigeonholed or put into a box. It is a fluid concept that changes in varying degrees from person to person throughout his or her lifetime.

Our local and global demographic landscape is changing at an alarming rate, with people gaining multiple cultural backgrounds as they move from one place to another and from one culture to another. My hope is that this book will encourage readers to question their own experiences of culture, past and present, and to explore how those experiences have shaped them and their lives. For some reason, this is an area that is neither heavily researched nor spoken about. I hope that this book will be a first step in that direction. The discussions about Chinese identity contained in this book are just the tip of the iceberg—the questions run so deep that they can't possibly be answered completely within one book. But hopefully this will open up branches of discussion between people and groups of people from many ethnic backgrounds, not just the Chinese. More than ever before, the topic and dynamics of cultural identity are relevant in the multicultural landscape of Canada.

The title of the book, No, Really, Where Are You From?, stems from my own frustrating experiences with trying to explain to people how a Chinese girl born in Venezuela ended up in Canada. Aside from my personal frustrations, however, I think it might actually be a good question for people to ask—with our demographic landscape changing so rapidly, perhaps people are just trying to catch up, trying to wrap their brains around the concepts of other cultures and ethnic identities that are foreign to them. And there is more to the question "No, really, where are you from?" than how other people see us—there is also the question of how we see ourselves.

When I told people that I was writing a book, and then told them the title, the most popular response I got was one of awkward silence. But I hope that once they've read the book, that silence will be replaced with lively and informative conversations between strangers, friends, families, organizations, schools, and politicians. And from there, as lofty of a goal as it may seem, I can only hope that there will be a shift in the human psyche toward some of the things our world seems to be struggling with: tolerance, understanding, and acceptance of others.

I hope that the experiences of all the people included in this book will resonate, in some way, with every person who reads it. But to fully understand and appreciate the experiences of these people, it might be helpful to understand, first, what historical events have led up to those experiences—to the very presence of Chinese people in lands so far away, both geographically and culturally, from China. It is with this in mind that I want to take a bit of time to talk about the history of Chinese immigration to Canada.

From Then To Now

Migration occurs because of a variety of circumstances, and it always comes with both opportunities and setbacks. And, while migration may seem like a relatively modern phenomenon, the truth is that, historically, the Chinese have always been migrant. This migration, however, increased substantially in the 19th century due to a number of factors.

In the 19th century, China experienced both war and famine, which forced many of its residents overseas. At the same time, the industrialized nations opened up opportunities for cheap labourers, thus attracting China's destitute. "The peak of Chinese out migrations occurred at the turn of the twentieth century, when massive numbers flowed out of China to all parts of the world during the 'coolie trade,' but Chinese migrations did not begin or end there" (Sowell 1996; Pan 1998: 65). As Kathleen Lopez writes, "migration is a network driven process: brothers followed brothers, sons followed sons, etc." (Beng, Storey et al. 2007:181).

There are pull and push factors involved in migration. Like most Canadian-born Chinese, modern day immigrants also find themselves being pulled from their traditional culture and pushed toward the mainstream culture of their adopted country. There is, in this, a tension or dual existence that becomes a metamorphosis—the new hybrid in a world where "heritage" involves multidimensional facets. The traditional Chinese culture is re-packaged as close as possible to its ancient ways in the new land, but it is significantly altered as well.

Some of the earliest Chinese immigrants came to Canada in the 1850s, during the Fraser River gold rush in British Columbia. And in the 1880s, Chinese labour was a major contributor to the building of the Canadian Pacific Railroad (Chow 1996: 23). During this period, Canada's immigration policy focused on the pragmatic and operated on a loosely monitored administration; it was only in the 20th century that visas, passports, and nation states were developed to help control migrant flows (Fleras & Elliot 1999). Prior to this, however, the primary concern of the state was land settlement (Richard 1991: 7), but settlement was generally restricted to "white" immigrants, and the Chinese were excluded from policies that sought to attract settlers with promises of free land. Instead, the Chinese were admitted into the country to meet a demand for short-term, unskilled labour. As with permanent settlers, immigration policy dictated the selection of permanent labourers based on racial and national origins. "In 1885, and again in 1902, a Royal Commission report stated that '… the importation into Canada of Chinese labor is not in the best interests of the country and should be prohibited…'" (Chow 1996:3).

This exclusion of the Chinese from groups that could be afforded permanent residence status reflected the dominant Canadian culture's fear and insecurity — that the Chinese would take jobs away from dominant groups (Chow 1996:3). Anti-Chinese organizations and societies, such as the Workingman's Protective Association, were established by the larger society as early as the 1870s (Chow 1996: 15). And this anxiety was also reflected in anti-Chinese legislations, which were created and passed by the Canadian government and supported by the wider Canadian society (Chow 1996:3). For example, in 1852, a "foreign miners' tax" was imposed on the Chinese, and in 1875, Chinese Canadians were stripped of the right to vote (Chow 1996:4). Further, the Chinese could not become citizens because federal law recognized only "white" persons as citizens (Takaki 1993:194). In 1885, a Head Tax of $50 per person was introduced, and this increased tenfold to $500 in 1904 (Chow 1996: 3). Sadly, many of the early Chinese immigrants who were required to pay the Head Tax have died and will never receive compensation. In 2006, compensation was finally granted to the handful of survivors. While many of their descendents do have current lawsuits against the Canadian federal government, there are also many who don't want to "rock the boat," for whatever reason.

When the federal government realized that the Head Tax wasn't achieving its desired effect (that is, stopping Chinese immigrants from coming to Canada), it implemented the Chinese Exclusion Act, with the sole intent of excluding, or at least curtailing, Chinese immigration. Ironically, this Act, which officially became law in 1923, was enacted on July 1st — Canada Day (Chow 1996: 4). The Act remained in effect until 1947 (Chow 1996: 138), only 65 years ago at the time of this writing.

Then, to add to the challenges that Chinese immigrants were already facing, laws were passed to restrict the immigration of Chinese women and to prevent immigrant men from bringing their wives over from China. How many lives and families this might destroy, how many hearts would be broken, was of no concern. The result was a "bachelor society" of Chinese men who spent the last years and days of their lives alone because those who were married couldn't have their wives with them. Though rare, intermarriages did occur (i.e. between First Nations women and Chinese men and between Scottish women and Chinese men).

These discriminatory legislations resulted in many of the early Chinese immigrants being driven into unemployment. And those who did find work were limited to low-paying jobs, occupational segregation, or self-employment. As Lily Chow explains, "it was very difficult for the Chinese people to find jobs because many mining companies, businesses and public works refused to employ them" (1996: 22). The mainstream Canadian ideology was one that drove the Chinese into subservient labour. Ronald Takaki writes, "they were also segregated within individual industries and paid less than white workers" (1993: 198). During hard economic times, the Chinese were both targeted and deeply resented by white Canadians.

There is little need to wonder why so many early immigrants wanted so desperately to return to China (although few had the means to do so). The antagonism and racism they faced was so great that they were often left with no choice but to try their hands at self-employment. Commonly, this self-employment would take the form of restaurants, stores, and laundromats because opening and running them required little starting capital, minimal skills, and little knowledge of the English language. What is interesting (and worrisome) is that laundromats, in particular, may have further reinforced the stereotype of the Chinese as a docile, subservient, and inferior people because this line of work has traditionally been regarded as "women's work." And women at that time were, of course, faced with many of these same stereotypes.

The majority of Chinese people migrating to Canada prior to 1923 had no knowledge of the English language, were rural-born, and were poorly educated (Con et al. 1982: 245). This, however, probably didn't have a significant impact on the lack of assimilation into Canadian culture because, at least during the late 1800s, even educated, Canadian-born Chinese people couldn't find meaningful work because of racist laws and views (Yee 1996:27).

Obviously, early Chinese Canadians, whether Chinese or Canadian born, faced an extraordinary amount of oppression. As Chow puts it, "they were often discouraged from coming ... and when they arrived, (they were) ghettoized and openly discriminated against" (1996: xiii). This would significantly impact the ability of Chinese Canadians to bridge the gap between the culture of the land of their origin and the culture of the new land.

The influence of the family in the socialization process is also a significant factor in preserving culture and cultural identity. But it's important to stress that the role of the family goes far beyond socialization — it also plays an important role throughout the life of an individual in the many aspects of and at different points in their lives. In other words, the particular impact a family has may vary within the ethnic community because socialization is only one of the many functions of the family. According to Anthony Richmond and Warren Kalbach, "as one of the most basic social units in Canadian society, the family plays a vital role in the socialization process and in the transmission of the family's cultural values and beliefs from one generation to the next" (1980:203). And, as Margaret Ward stresses, "parents are the single most powerful influence in the socialization of their children" (1998:151).

Socializing agents from the larger society (such as childcare, peers, schools, media, etc.) also play a vital role in preserving or diluting the ethnic identity of the individual (Ward 1998). While the family passes on the ethnic culture to the individual, the school (as a feature of the host society) passes on the culture of the host country (Mancho 1982). Thus, the socializing agent that has the most influential role in an individual's life will also have the greatest impact on preservation of ethnic identity. So, for instance, if the school plays the most influential role, there would likely be a higher rate of assimilation and a lower rate of ethnic identity retention. It's important to note that this is more likely to occur when the individual enters the educational system as a child. The younger the child is, the more time he or she is likely to spend in the educational system.

Through these processes, the child may be torn between embracing either the culture of origin or the host culture (Gokalp 1988). Further, where the child is educated will vary, depending on the availability of ethnic schools and whether the family can afford the tuition at such schools. Thus, socio-economic status and the institutions of the ethnic community also come into play. This is also true, to some extent, for adults who attend language classes either in their own community or the wider community.

And, of course, if the family is the major socializing agent, then ethnic identity retention also depends on what is defined as "important" by the family and whether that definition includes assimilation into the dominant culture. Other factors, such as the number of children in a family and the presence or absence of extended family members, also impact the socialization process.

An excellent example of how the structure of an ethnic community impacts cultural retention is explained by Raymond Breton's concept of the "institutional completeness" (the degree to which the ethnic group has developed formal structures and organizations to serve the needs of its members within the ethnic community) of an ethnic group. In his significant 1964 article, Breton argues that institutional completeness keeps the immigrants' social relations within ethnic boundaries, thus heightening their ethnic identity. This is significant in that the greater the institutional completeness of a group, the more likely individuals in that group will maintain allegiances, and the majority of the relationships they form will be with other members of the same group. The author does argue, however, that institutional completeness is more successful in some ethnic communities than it is in others. And the degree of institutional completeness can also vary even within a specific ethnic community.

Madeline Kalbach (2000) argues that interracial marriage is also an important indicator of assimilation. As intermarriages would have allowed for more opportunities to incorporate into the larger society, the prohibition of intermarriages (as a feature of the larger society) between the early Chinese and white settlers in Canada was another critical factor in delaying assimilation and maintaining stronger cultural retention amongst the early Chinese.

These are just some of the important factors, according to past research, that contribute to, or detract from, assimilation. It's important, however, to consider how these factors function within a changed economic context. That is, how does the global economy modify (or does it modify) the impact of these individual features?

Minako K. Maykovich argues that contemporary Chinese immigrants who are "coming with status equal to that of the members of the host society rapidly become integrated into the host society on social and cultural levels" (1976: 385). If Maykovich is correct, then we would expect that an elite group of Chinese immigrants would assimilate quickly into mainstream Canadian society. According to Lloyd Wong, many contemporary Chinese have a high level of education, are proficient in English, and are very affluent (1997: 342). According to Kay Anderson, "the majority of Chinese-origin immigrants to Canada after 1967 came directly from Hong Kong, where many had acquired English-language education and lived a decade or more in an urban environment not altogether alien to the industrial West" (1991:214).

Because contemporary Chinese immigrants have a higher education level than the early immigrants did, there are more opportunities for them to have close friends amongst the Canadian-born population. Contemporary immigrants are also more equipped to participate in mainstream activities because they often don't face the language barriers that make communication and social interaction difficult. And even for immigrants who don't have English language skills, it is still likely that they have a fairly high level of education in general. And the level of education at entry has always been found to be the key to successful economic, cultural, and social integration of immigrants not fluent in English or French (Richmond 1967).

The fact that the educated Chinese of today interact to a much greater degree with people from mainstream society also impacts the rate of intermarriages. According to Jay Goldstein and Alexander Segall, there has been an increase in the rate of intermarriages, and "sociologists have tended to view ethnic intermarriage as posing problems for the maintenance of ethnic identity" (1991:165). Or, in other words, intermarriage encourages assimilation.

When we look at all of these factors collectively, we see a dichotomy between early and contemporary Chinese immigrants. The early Chinese immigrants were usually English illiterate and poorly educated, which led to them being isolated from mainstream society (Con et al. 1982:152). They also were more likely than their contemporary counterparts to belong to ethnic "clubs," which resulted in a slower process of assimilation and a higher degree of cultural retention. Contemporary immigrants, on the other hand, are generally highly educated and integrate much more quickly into mainstream society. But the flip side of that is that they, unlike the early immigrants, tend to experience a lower degree of cultural retention.

There is one more feature of the Chinese population that I would like to talk about briefly, because it seems so often to come into play in the stories of the people in this book. That is the work ethic that the Chinese are so famous for.

Picture the 1950s Chinese Cultural Revolution lead by Mao Tse Tung, or — as he is more famously known as — Chairman Mao. Even in the generations prior to this time, there was a lot of political corruption in China. And, unlike many western nations, China never had a welfare system. There was never a social net of government support, as my father and grandfather often reminded me. Prior to marrying, the children stayed home and looked after their parents. And even after marriage, the oldest son remained responsible for the care of his parents. There was no such thing as a nursing home in China. Family members would often strategize together to form a family business so that they could look after everyone in the family. And they would only very rarely hire "outsiders."

It's not uncommon to see the remnants of this cultural inheritance even today. Often a wife will go live with her new husband's family to look after his parents. Arranged marriages and the marrying of daughters to wealthier families are not unheard of and have their roots in economic convenience. And, as calculating and insensitive as the economic convenience view may seem, it's important to remember that it stems, in large part, from the Chinese forefathers' desperate measures to survive in an uncertain environment. In essence, we see Charles Darwin's theory of adaptation at play here.

Knowing that the early Chinese immigrants pounded stake after stake of the Canadian Pacific Railway and chiseled the frozen Rocky Mountains in British Columbia over 200 years ago, all to the benefit of future generations of Canadians, should be a cause of great pride. It is, after all, the hard work ethic of these Chinese men that connected an entire country. And knowing this, it's tempting to be not only embittered, but also mystified by the racism that these men faced. The truth is, however, that the Chinese are hardly alone in having faced this type of discrimination.

It's difficult for any visible minority to avoid racism and discrimination. Although there may be less discrimination today, it is also possible that it's just more subtle. It other words, the situation may not really be "better"; it could be that racism itself hasn't really been significantly reduced — it's just more polite. And if racism has not been eradicated in the past, it's not likely to go away anytime soon. What we can hope for, however, is that our children today are more educated in the importance of acceptance and cultural diversity. After all, our demographic landscape has changed dramatically in just the last 50-60 years. The local has become the global.

The world is changing, and people have broader views. People are travelling more, and we see more and more Chinese entering the professions previously denied to non-white immigrants to Canada. Unlike the poor Chinese immigrants of 200 years ago, we are seeing more contemporary Chinese people in the upper economic class. And many of these people are wealthy for no other reason than that they worked hard, brought that hard work ethic with them to the new land, and eventually passed down that ethic from one generation to the next (if the next generation accepted it).

And so there is much to celebrate about the Chinese heritage in Canada and even more to talk about as the Chinese community continues to evolve. And part of that is to move the issues from the universal to the individual, where we can learn from personal stories and experiences, and from the academic to the emotional, where we learn how real people are impacted physically, psychologically, and emotionally by the push and pull between cultures. Unfortunately, along with strong work ethic often comes the idea that survival always trumps constitutional and personal rights. And the idea of talking about how one "feels" can be a foreign concept in the Chinese community.

But talk we must. And talk we will. That, in the end, is what this book is all about. So let the stories begin.

Señorita Maracay

The theme of Chinese identity runs prevalent throughout this book, regardless of where the individual in question was born. I myself was born in Maracay, Venezuela—nowhere near Canada or China. Nevertheless, I am of Chinese descent. I spent the first seven years of my life in Venezuela before immigrating to Canada and living most of my life in Edmonton, Alberta.

Venezuela is located at the northern tip of South America, with the northern part of the country embraced by the Caribbean Sea. For the first seven years of my life, that sea was my backyard. I still often long for Venezuela, and it is perhaps that longing, and my continued attachment to the Spanish culture, that inspired me to name my chapter "Señorita Maracay" a nickname that the German owner of a hostel I stayed in on a trip to Venezuela in 2007 gave me upon hearing that I had been born in Maracay.

Maracay is about a 45-minute drive from Caracas, the capital of Venezuela, and is a military town with a lot of colonial influences. It's also the cradle of Venezuela's aviation industry. This town, where I began my life, is the setting for a lot of my fondest memories. In particular, I remember an elderly neighbor who was always kind to me and took care of me—oddly enough, although he was almost like a father to me, I've forgotten his name. I will never, however, forget his kindness.

There are also many other events in my life that have stayed with me, whether they happened in Venezuela or in Canada. But first, I want to go back even further—to events that made my existence and my memories possible.

My grandfather, Chai Ten Ng, immigrated to Venezuela from China in 1934 because of the destitute economic conditions in China at the time. With a new life in a new country and culture, came his new Spanish name: Julio Ng. Julio stayed in Venezuela for five years before returning to China to give it another try. This lasted for ten years, at which point he returned to Venezuela and never saw China again.

Julio Ng, in Venezuela, 1956

My grandfather had no family in Venezuela, just a few friends who were from the same Chinese village as him. His wife and children all remained in China and waited for him to send money back home. My grandfather had no formal education, little money, and didn't know a single word of Spanish. I sometimes wonder if he even knew where exactly Venezuela was or what he was getting himself into. But, regardless of what he knew or didn't know, he persevered and eventually thrived in Venezuela.

He began supporting himself in his new life by buying pastries at a bakery and going to bus stations to sell them right off of the cookie sheets they were baked on. Eventually, he got a job in a small coffee shop doing whatever was needed — washing dishes, serving, or cooking (I can't resist interrupting myself here to say that he was the best cook I've ever known). Although he made very little money, he always sent money home to his family in China, leaving himself very little to live on. He lived in rooming houses with shared facilities, and his bed was usually a mattress he found in the garbage. When the mattress got too flat from wear and tear, he would put luggage underneath it to give it some support. Sometimes, he didn't have enough money to even pay for a bus and would walk home from work in the cold. He often went without food.

In spite of this, my grandfather managed to eventually save enough money to go into partnership and co-own a coffee shop, which brought its own difficulties. Racist comments, customers stiffing him on the bill, and potential fights with customers were part of his daily life in Venezuela.

So there he was, alone in a strange country for years, working 12 to 13 hour days every day. When I think of him now, my heart breaks for every discriminated behaviour towards him. And I think that he must have been scared — how could he not be? But he, like so many immigrants, suppressed his daily pain and persevered for the sake of his family and their future.

Hardships aside, the letters my grandfather sent back to China were enough to stir a fire within my father and persuade him to also seek adventure in a foreign land. Eventually, my grandfather sponsored my father—whom he had not seen in ten years by this point—to come to Venezuela.

Santiago Ng, 15 years old, in Cuba, en route to Venezuela.

Born in the Chinese province of Guangdong, my father, Kin Ling Ng, was 15 when he made the journey to Venezuela in the mid-1950s, and he would spend a large part of his life there. Like my grandfather and so many Chinese who immigrated to Venezuela, my father has a Spanish name: Santiago. I remember my father telling me that when he first arrived in Venezuela, after a decade of not seeing my grandfather, both were not sure if one would recognize the other. It seemed like an awkward interaction.

When he was 23 or 24, my father went to Hong Kong for his arranged marriage with Anna (my biological mother). They established a life in Venezuela.

By 1965, my father was a successful businessman who owned and operated a supermarket, "Supermecardo Occidental," in Maracay. He ran that business for 20 years, and with the money he made, he helped bring most of the rest of his family from China to Venezuela. This act and his business acumen made him somewhat of a hero to both his extended family and the community as a whole. But as "big" as my father was to family, the community, or the supermarket business, he was simply papi (Spanish for "dad") to me.

Of my siblings and me, I am the only one with any real childhood memories of Venezuela, and the majority of those memories involve my father in some way because I spent most of my time with him. My older sister lived in Hong Kong with my grandparents during most of this time, and my younger sister and brother were very young when we had moved to Canada.

On May 5th, 1977, the day we arrived in Edmonton, my world turned upside down—at least from my perspective as a seven-year-old child. For the next four or five years, I hardly saw my father because he was travelling back and forth between Canada and Venezuela, where he still had to tend to the supermarket. I grew resentful of my father because I missed him so much. But I was so young that I couldn't articulate that; I just knew that I wanted him around.

But it wasn't only his presence I missed—it was also his protection. My mother, Anna, was psychologically unstable, and when my father wasn't around, she would tell me daily that I didn't really "belong" in the family and would remind me constantly that she had the power to toss me out onto the streets. Although this began even before we moved to Canada, the situation intensified after we immigrated. Because of the abuse I suffered at her hands, I have never been able to call her "mother" and certainly not "mom." "Anna" is the most I have ever been able to manage.

Almost every day for ten years, I was teased, belittled, and humiliated. I was the target of snide remarks and vicious rumours initiated by either Anna or my siblings, whom Anna trained to treat me with the same derision that she did. Without my father around, Anna held an authoritative role, and she was quick to take advantage of that. As for me—how could I not listen to the person who was feeding me? I was overweight as a child due to a thyroid medication I was on, and that same medication made me prone to fatigue. This became a weapon to be used against me. I was the "fat" one or the "lazy" one in the family.

By the time I was a teenager, I was even more resentful of what I saw as my father's neglect. By this time, the business he had started in Chinatown was failing, and he was so consumed by that that he never really noticed what was going on at home. Although I understand now that, while he may not have been the "best" parent, he did the best he could. And I know now that he was in turmoil himself. And when he was there, he was a good father. But for the most part, I felt like an orphan.

During this difficult period in my life, I had the fortunate opportunity to spend more time with my grandfather and I got to know him much better. My grandparents took care of us some times when my dad was busy tending to the store in Chinatown. I have strong fond memories of going to my grandfather's townhouse for lunch (and sometimes dinner too) while I was attending junior high school. We were never a burden to him. I still recall him encouraging us to go over to his home for supper even when we didn't need to.

So, for all intents and purposes, I had no immediate family in Canada (other than my father from time to time and my grandfather). And what extended family I had (or still have) left little to no impression on me because we have never spent time together—I see them only at weddings or funerals. This is in contrast to Venezuela, where I do remember being surrounded by aunts, uncles, cousins, and other relatives. But even in Venezuela, I don't remember ever celebrating the Chinese New Year, although we did celebrate the "regular" New Year by setting off fireworks right outside of our home (yes, it was legal!) in Maracay. In general, I don't think we ever celebrated our Chinese heritage, at least not to nearly the same degree we celebrated the Spanish culture. I remember having birthday parties where we would strike, blindfolded, at a candy-and-trinket-stuffed piñata until it burst and spilled its treasures out on the ground.

When I lived in Venezuela, the Chinese population was very, very small. And so the only Chinese people I ever interacted with were related to me in one way or another. In Canada, the equation flipped: I had very little family, but there were substantially more Chinese people in the general population. What didn't change was my exposure to the Chinese culture; although there were other Chinese families in the neighbourhood we lived in, my family never socialized or interacted with them. The Chinese culture didn't play a big role in my life. But the Venezuelan Spanish culture did—from the food to the people to the language to the dance. I don't remember ever having a struggle with culture in Venezuela. But as a newly arrived youngster in Edmonton, I didn't really feel like I had a true affiliation with any particular culture. I wasn't Spanish because I didn't live in Venezuela anymore. I wasn't Canadian because I didn't look Canadian. And I wasn't Chinese because I didn't feel Chinese.

Somehow, in spite of these conditions, I did speak Cantonese while I was growing up. And, amazingly, I have managed to hold on to a lot of it (no small miracle considering that my first language is actually Spanish, which I haven't been quite so successful at holding onto, mostly because of a lack of opportunity to practice it. The only other person I know who speaks Spanish is my father). My Cantonese certainly isn't great, but it works well enough to get me by, although it always takes me a few moments to switch gears between languages. Without my father, I have my nephew Max and my niece Julia to practice Cantonese with, however, I never would have managed to keep up with the language. Often, when I hear Julia (who was 11 years old at the time this book was written) speaking English, I pretend that I don't understand her just so we are both forced to communicate in Cantonese. The dialect I also speak with my father and my grandfather (when he was alive) is from Heung ha. Heung ha is not the name of a place, it means "native village." My grandfather and father spoke literally in their village dialect.

In Maracay, I attended a school called Instituto Escuela Maracay. Of course, I attended only the first grade before moving to Canada. But that one year of school in Venezuela left a huge impression on me.

I'm pretty sure that my sister and I were the only Chinese students at that school, and I remember it being a peaceful place where I was never teased or bullied and never experienced racism. My father has told me, though, that it was quite common for me to come home from school crying because I wanted to be a little black girl. I don't, however, have any memory of that and can only assume that I just wanted to look like the other students, who were mostly black, mulatto, or European Spanish. But I think this desire stemmed more from a feeling of solidarity than it did from a feeling of being ostracized.

On the other hand, I definitely remember feeling awkward and as though I didn't fit in once we moved to Canada. And even though there were other Chinese students in the school I attended, I felt uncomfortable with them as well. Here I was, in a cold place with snow, no water, sand, or mangoes in sight and all the people looked so different from what I was used to. I remember feeling like my world had turned upside down; I found it really hard to relate to the people around me, regardless of their cultural backgrounds.

I was a very shy and quiet girl when I was young, and this was a very confusing time for me. What few friends I did manage to make were Caucasians, and it wouldn't be until junior high that I made any friends from different cultural backgrounds (such as Lebanese and Fijian).

When I was young, my father showed little interest in my schooling. I never really understood why, but recently, I came to find out that he associated education with death. He had an older brother who was a highly educated engineer. In 1959, that brother, on one of his days off from work, went inside of a machine (my father never specified what kind of a machine) to check on it. While he was still inside, someone turned the machine on, and my father's brother was killed. At the time, my father and grandfather were both in Venezuela — my father was 19 or 20 years old, and his life changed forever. In the blink of an eye, he became the sole surviving son (a younger brother died in childhood) in his family, and the expectations put on him as a son and a brother were incredible.

My uncle's death was so tragic and devastating that my father still has a hard time talking about it. He sometimes tells me about how he would watch my grandfather cry in the kitchen of the restaurant. Ever since that event, my father — and probably my grandfather — had associated education with death. If my uncle was not so educated, the reasoning goes, he would not have gone into that machine, and he would not have been killed. And, as irrational as that may sound, the connection is very real to my father. When my father told me this story, it suddenly became clear to me why he didn't want to me to go to Ottawa to complete my Master's degree. It wasn't that he didn't want me to better myself — he was simply afraid of losing me. I am happy to say, however, that my father has since softened on this point and is very proud of my academic achievements.

As with most people from a visible minority, I experienced my share of racism as well. Between being Chinese, overweight, shy, and quiet, I was an easy target. Other students would call me names and wait for me after school so they could torment me, even following me home and harassing me the entire time. I particularly remember one incident when I was in junior high: at the time, I played the flute in music class. One day, a group of bullies decided to gang up on me. In my mind's eye, I can still see how the flute case I was carrying flew out of my hand and scraped across the gravel road as the bullies pushed me back and forth between them. These types of events only added to my feelings of worthlessness.

When I entered my teenage years, I became more and more distant from everyone and everything. Although my father, by that time, was starting to spend longer periods of time in Canada because he had decided to build and operate a huge grocery store in Edmonton's Chinatown, the deep recession of the early and mid-1980s took its toll, and he was forced to sell the business after only three years. At this point he started to fall into a depression. For a man who had run a successful business for almost 20 years, was instrumental in bringing all of his family over from China to Venezuela, and had raised a family of his own, this failure was a huge blow. I, of course, didn't know that at the time—and I doubt very much that he wanted me, or anyone for that matter, to know. It was far too important to him to maintain his image and "keep face." In the Chinese culture it is simply unacceptable to show any sign of weakness.

And even if there had been signs, I doubt that I would have noticed them—I was falling apart myself by then. I had an enlarged thyroid gland that was wreaking havoc with my physical health. Between the thyroid problem and the medication I was on to treat it, I suffered from symptoms ranging from weight gain to fatigue to depression. In hindsight, I'm sometimes surprised that I'm not completely illiterate. I certainly had no interest in school, and I struggled constantly to pay attention in class. My marks in high school were nothing short of dismal. The medication I was on was simply too much for me, but no one noticed or did anything about it. And the stress of my home life being, to put it bluntly, a living hell, certainly didn't help.

Not surprisingly, given my health and my home situation, I didn't care much about, or even give any thought to, anything related to being Chinese. I just knew that I didn't want to be anything like the rest of my family. I would dye my hair blonde and refused to make friends with other Chinese people — they reminded me too much of my family. I also developed a deep independent streak, and this went against the Chinese tradition of female dependence. I witnessed how most of the other Chinese women I knew disregarded the value of education and responded to the beck and call of the men around them, who would, supposedly, take care of them for life. At times, it seemed to me like I was watching something from the 1800s. I knew I didn't want this for my life, so I was determined to be different. And I've kept that promise.

In a twisted way, Anna's abuse inspired me to be better than her and to fight for my independence. As bad as things got, I never let myself slip into something that I couldn't recover from. I was never an addict or an alcoholic, never had an unplanned pregnancy, never ran away from home or became a prostitute, or did other such things that would have proven that I was what Anna had said I was all along. Instead, I worked hard at proving her wrong. And the older I got, the more I noticed the correlation between my success and her abuse. The more successful I became, the angrier she was. At times, I felt like I was living in a nuclear plant marinated in toxic chemicals, dying little by little.

Eventually, and not surprisingly, Anna had kicked me out of the house. Even though she instigated my leave, it's not lost on me that it was a communal decision. That was quite a pivotal and profound moment in my young life. Considering the life long abuse from Anna and the spineless loyalty to her by my siblings, I had made a life altering decision. I decided they would never be a part of my life again. I have kept that promise to this day, and life has been toxic free for the most part. The abuse began in my infancy and built up over 20 years, so going through life without them was not a very difficult decision to make. Without them, I thrived, blossomed and found a love for life and a sense of purpose that I had never experienced before. To this day, I still don't have a relationship with Anna, and I don't expect that I ever will.

The most important relationship to me is the one I have with my father, and when my grandfather was alive, he and my father were the 2 most important people in my life. When I was in my early twenties, my father opened a laundromat on a property he owned. I was going to school in the same neighbourhood as the laundromat and lived close by as well. When I could, I helped him at the laundromat, and it was during those years that we started talking a lot. And my father would tell me stories—stories about Venezuela, stories about China, and stories about my ancestors.

One of the stories he told me was about my great grandfather (my paternal grandmother's father), who immigrated in the late 1800s or early 1900s to Canada to work on the railroad. While he was in Victoria, British Columbia, he won a lottery and immediately did what so many of the early immigrants longed to do—he returned to China. But upon his return to China, the Cultural Revolution came about, creating huge problems for him. Because my great grandfather was a landlord, he was targeted by both the Chinese government and the Red Guards. He was falsely accused of owning and harbouring weapons.

Because he didn't actually have these weapons, he was, of course, unable to produce them. But the accusations and demands continued. Tragically, the pressures eventually became unbearable for him, and he took his own life. My grandmother, my father said, was never the same again.

It was stories like these that inspired me to ask more questions, and I began to appreciate my Chinese heritage. Of course, I was in my twenties at the time, so I was pretty absorbed in mainstream culture, and I still put those influences ahead of the Chinese ones. But I now had a curiosity about my heritage that I never had when I was younger. Hearing about the struggles that my father and grandfather went through opened up my mind and heart to the culture I had been shutting out of my life. And opening my heart and mind to that culture is what led me to complete my Master's degree in Sociology and, ultimately, to write this book.

All of the research that went into my Master's degree and into this book had a huge impact on my cultural identity. For one thing, I began to realize how my Chinese heritage had already affected me, whether I knew it or not. For instance, I have definitely inherited the Chinese work ethic from my father and grandfather. I typically have a lot of things on my plate at once, such as juggling two jobs, volunteering, and researching and writing. When I look at it from a distance, it seems like an insane lifestyle, but for me it's just second nature.

I also began to really see and appreciate cultural influences and how they were present, or absent, in my life. With every interview I conducted for the book, I learned a little bit more about the Chinese culture, and I was able to sort through different aspects of it and decide what I did and didn't agree with. For instance, I have a hard time wrapping my head around the idea of "vertical respect". While I certainly believe it's important to respect my elders, I believe that everybody is deserving of that same kind of respect. I also don't agree with the belief that children should be "seen and not heard:" I believe that everyone should have the chance to be heard. I also don't agree with the idea that Chinese girls are of little relevance to the family and that they exist on the bottom rung of the "vertical respect" ladder. And I certainly don't believe that I need to pursue and marry a wealthy Chinese man who will take care of me for the rest of my life.

I am not, nor have I ever been, married. While it's hard for me to say with certainty that my life journey has directly influenced my choice in the cultural background of my significant other, I suspect that it has.

When I was growing up, I felt a definite pressure to marry another Chinese person. It was, however, an unspoken pressure. Only one member of my family that I know of, a cousin of mine, has ever married a non Chinese person. While I don't remember any huge outcry or explicit disapproval of that marriage, there were a lot of whispers about a relative's disapproval of her new daughter-in-law, and how the relative couldn't communicate with her interracial grandchildren. So, although there wasn't an outright spoken "ban" on interracial marriage in my family, I certainly felt the thick tension regarding the issue.

I have yet to decide what disturbs me most—the unspoken or the direct belief that we are to "stick to our own kind." I do know, however, that I bought into that whole belief for about a minute. And then I rejected it. I have never dated a Chinese man and in general, I don't find myself attracted to Chinese men. I'm not exactly sure why, although I suspect it has something to do with many of the same reasons that I had only non Chinese friends while I was growing up. Also, the Chinese beliefs and traditions weren't drilled into my head from a young age—partly because I was more immersed in the Spanish culture, and partly because I never really had a stable and secure childhood or family-like environment to grow up in. The Chinese influence came to me only later in my life, and by then I had developed into a very self sufficient, independent woman. I had come to know that these are not very desirable qualities in a Chinese wife, from my family and from the older, more traditional Chinese culture. On the other hand, the educated, younger, and modern generations would see these qualities as appealing.

Perhaps I have just become too conditioned to thinking of Chinese marriage as being associated only with economic convenience and financial status as opposed to true love and respect. The one time I was pursued by a Chinese man wasn't a very pleasant experience for me. No matter how many times or in how many ways I told this man that I wasn't interested or that I had a boyfriend, he wouldn't stop. And when he found out how financially appealing my home was, he became even more desperate, obsessive, and aggressive—bringing meals to my work, sending me gifts, calling me by nicknames I never appreciated, and talking constantly about "how appealing our net worth would be if we got together" and how he was going to own a BMW car in the future. This was 7 years ago. The last I heard, he is still driving the same beat up old car. Although I never gave him any indication that I was even remotely interested, he would bring up marriage. "A marriage," he would say, "stands half a chance of survival if the union is in good financial standing." He didn't seem to have any inkling that he was making me feel like a meal ticket. At the time, I didn't really understand his fixation on money—or on me—but after conducting one particular interview in this book, it finally dawned on me: Based on my personal experience and from the interviews with the older Chinese people, my definition of a traditional Chinese marriage is about—economic convenience. Look for a wealthy mate. While that helped me understand the behaviors of this particular man a bit better, it made me even more determined to not get caught in a traditional Chinese marriage.

Perhaps he was raised with old Chinese traditions and beliefs on marriage, and he's simply doing what has been taught to him. This is not to say that I am attributing his behavior towards marriage to Chinese traditional ideology. There are other cultures or individuals, throughout history and even today, whereby marriage is strictly based on economic relief. For instance, during England's medieval period, and not as predominant today in modern England, marrying into the right class was the ultimate goal (a great example is the movie, The Duchess (2008) with Keira Knightley). If we look at the modern day East Indian culture, we find many arranged marriages amongst young and modern people.

I would like to know that I am valued for more than my money (if I have any), that my opinions matter, and that there is substance in my relationship. Perhaps I have seen too many Chinese wives walking behind their husbands. Or, too many Chinese women who blow off opportunities for education because they're waiting for a man to "save" them and a marriage will spring them up a few notches on the food chain.

Don't get me wrong—I'm not saying that the Chinese culture is horrible, or even wrong, in its insistence that Chinese people should marry only other Chinese people. Please also know that if I come across as painting all Chinese people as money hungry gold diggers, it was never my intention. I've come to understand that a lot of this thought process comes more from the older Chinese generation, since this is not the case amongst modern Chinese populations around the world. But, there is certainly something to be said for the idea that in order to maintain a culture and have it hold through generations you must keep the ethnic group that carries the culture "intact." What I'm uncomfortable with is how this means, then, that that community then becomes more important than the individual. I can't seem to negotiate the collective philosophy of the East with the individualistic philosophy of the West. I've witnessed what can happen when you become so much a product of your culture that you lose yourself and become a shell of a person because social acceptance ("keeping face"), rather than personal needs (not just wants, mind you, but needs) has become the main motivating factor in your life. It broke my heart to see my father struggle and disintegrate under the intense and toxic pressures and burden of the Chinese culture. I know what comes with the territory.

But this isn't to say that I don't see any value in the Chinese culture, and I'm currently involved in a lot of activities related to being Chinese. The Chinese culture, of course, takes centre stage in my research and in my writing, and I'm passionate about passing what I learn on to others. One of my goals is to tweak and polish a play I've written—The Yellow Peril—about the experiences of early Chinese immigrants in Canada and submit a proposal to my local school board to have it become part of the social studies curriculum. My hope is to leave a lasting impression on students that will go beyond the line (or two, if we're lucky) about Canadian-Chinese history that's found in current textbooks.

I love traditional Chinese food—although I don't necessarily like cooking it. Then again, I don't like cooking, period. My father and I also try to keep up the tradition of going for dim sum. My father is an avid reader of the Chinese newspaper, and I try to take a peek every now and then.

I continue to speak Cantonese with my family. And, although I don't have children, my niece and nephew do attend Chinese school on Saturdays. And this is a tradition I would follow if I did have children. Even if my children rebelled against it, I think I would ensure that they absorbed that part of the culture rather than having them grow up regretting that they had not done so. I believe that the Chinese language is more than just language—it's also a key to opening up doors to the past and to the future. I believe that speaking Chinese gives me a sense of groundedness, an anchor, regardless of what is going on in my life.

I do think that my educational status and occupations have had an influence on the retention and loss of my Chinese identity. It's a bit of a paradox. On the one hand, it's unusual for a Chinese person to study the arts and humanities, and many traditional Chinese may not even know exactly what Sociology is. Thus, choosing this path has meant that I have less exposure to other Chinese people. In the department where I work for my full-time job, there are very few Asian people. Perhaps there are more Asians working in other departments or there are generally less Asians working within the public. As for my part time job at a major grocery store chain, I'm not exposed to a lot of other Chinese workers or Chinese customers either. This may be due to the fact that not a lot of Chinese people live in the area. This is not to say that the other store locations are the same, and it may have more Asian workers and customers. For instance, the grocery chain (as well as other grocery chains) I work for has not successfully integrated the new economic model of selling Asian grocery items and thus, the customers will shop somewhere else. Also, if I worked in a store that catered specifically to selling Chinese/Asian goods, then I would be exposed to more Chinese workers and customers.

On the other hand, Sociology has opened so many doors into the Chinese world for me. The intense research I've done and the strong interest I have in Chinese heritage has arisen primarily out of my graduate and undergraduate years in university.

A trip to Asia in 2009 brought me even closer to my cultural heritage. On this trip, I explored exotic Thailand, warm Cambodia, and amazing China. What can I say about my impressions of China? I was surprised by so many things, such as the lack of rice paddies and the quantity of corn crops around Beijing. I was also surprised by how many Chinese tourists there were. When I was at the Forbidden City, it was packed with Chinese people. I remember thinking, "Why are they not at work? Why are they here?" I had somehow expected that all, or at least the majority, of the tourists would be foreigners, not locals. But what I failed to consider is how big the country actually is: of course not everyone is from Beijing, and there is probably still an entire generation of Chinese nationals and foreign born Chinese, such as myself, who haven't seen this breathtaking palace.

Another surprise for me was the food. I have to admit that I was uncomfortable with eating during my trip. What I thought was pork dumpling didn't taste like pork, and I was afraid that any sort of meat I put in my mouth might actually be dog, cat, or rat meat. I was also uncomfortable with the huge throngs of people that I'm not accustomed to encountering in spacious Canada. And the lack of hygienic restrooms also made me shudder. Actually, this might have bothered me the most because I knew, from my research, that the Chinese government spent billions of dollars to build the biggest dam in the world (the Three Gorges Dam), so I couldn't understand why they couldn't invest a bit more in ensuring that their people had access to proper hygiene.

But there were also a lot of things that I loved about China. My dream to see and walk on one of the great wonders of the world—the Great Wall of China—finally came true. And I will never forget the sight of the Terracotta Warriors in Xian. This spectacle truly took my breath away. I also finally got the chance to travel along the Yangtze River, to feel the haunting spirits of those millions of Chinese people who lost their homes and their livelihoods in the name of progress. Because I was familiar with the fascinating and tragic life of China's last emperor Pu Yi, as portrayed in the 1988 Oscar-winning movie, The Last Emperor, my visit to the Forbidden City was even more meaningful than it would have been otherwise. The big red doors of the palace left me speechless and in awe. As I explored the alleys in and around the palace, I could have sworn I felt the presence of the spirit of Pu Yi as a little boy.

I also can't claim that my experiences of racism have been limited to Canada. When I returned to Venezuela for a visit in 2007, I was in one of the souvenir shops at the airport when one of the workers said to me in Spanish (probably assuming that I wouldn't understand her), "What can I do for you, Chinese?" Although my knowledge of Spanish is limited, I knew enough to respond to her. "My name is not Chinese," I said. "My name is Nancy." I can't really explain the look on her face, except to say that it was priceless.

I wish I could say that I never again encountered racism as an adult, but unfortunately that's not the case. About 10 years ago and shortly after I started working for the public sector, I was sitting in the lunchroom during a coffee break reading the paper when a co-worker came in. After realizing that we were the only people in the room, she began asking me about what I took in school. When I told her about my research on Chinese-Canadian history, she proceeded to tell me, bitterly, "all Chinese people should go back where they belong."

Naturally, I was bothered by this, and brought it to my boss's attention. My boss, in turn, reported it to upper management. I came to find out later that this person and I had applied for the same position, and I had been given the position while she had been passed over for it. At that point, I thought that her comment was just sour grapes, and probably had little to do with an ingrained racist attitude. What baffled me is that an ex-boyfriend had said the same thing to me while we were dating. That's why he's an EX-boyfriend now. Coincidence? Maybe. But it also makes me wonder if there are a lot of other people out there saying (or at least thinking) the same thing.

Another example of where I see subtle racism is when people I know are involved in car accidents, and when they relay the story of the accident, they insist on telling me that the other driver was a member of a visible minority. While I certainly empathize with their pain, and (although I've never been in a major car accident) I can sympathize with the inconvenience and the physical and emotional impact of being in a car accident, I'm always at a loss as to understand what the ethnicity of the other driver has to do with anything. I have never heard anyone specify that the driver of the other car had blue eyes or red hair. The suggestion seems to be that people of a visible minority are inherently bad drivers or trouble makers.

It would seem that there are still instances of racism all around us, whether they are subtle or direct. Fortunately for me, it didn't take me too long to figure out that I wasn't the problem, and that racism usually stems from the insecurities and frustrations of the people committing the racist behaviour. Insecurities and frustrations that they take out on other people. For the most part, I have learned over the years to not take racism personally and to remove myself from these situations — just as I learned that I needed to remove myself from Anna's abuse.

I do believe, however, that the level of tolerance for the Chinese has improved drastically in the last few decades. I see this in the media, in the growth of Edmonton's Chinatown, and in the appointment of the first Chinese Lieutenant Governor of Alberta, Norman Kwong. The growth has been slow, but impressive and progressive. There are, of course, still subtle forms of racism directed toward the Chinese community every day — and there probably always will be, even if one day our Prime Minister happens to be of Chinese descent. There are definitely times when the colour of people's skin is given more importance than their character or credentials, and that upsets me as well.

When I was young, I didn't give any thought to any kind of identity — for me, those years were mostly just about survival. But in the last 15 or 20 years, I've grown to be very proud of my Chinese heritage. I am still, however, working on the "Canadian" part of my identity. I definitely experienced a cultural identity crisis because of growing up in two very different countries and with three very different cultures. And there must be some truth to what they say about a child's most formative years being the first five because, for me, even though I've spent much more time living in Canada than I did in Venezuela, Venezuela still feels like "home." My heart beats faster when I hear someone speaking in Spanish. Hearing the Spanish words is like a spirit calling out to me. Of course, it could also have to do with the fact that I remember so clearly being happy in Venezuela, whereas most of my childhood memories from Canada are harsh and painful. But whatever the reason, as unpatriotic as it may sound (and my deepest apologies to fans of hockey, beer, poutine, and beaver tails!) Canada often feels to me like it's just a place where I have a job and a house to return to after a vacation. My heart, however, has always been and always will be in Venezuela. They don't call me Señorita Maracay for nothing!

A Soup Called Love

It's noon, and, as usual, I'm returning to the office after lunch. As I enter the office, I'm overwhelmed by the aroma of soup. The soup is Susan's, and it's delicious. I know this because the smell reminds me of the years my grandfather cooked for me and my siblings. My grandfather was a great cook. No matter what he made for us, we always thought it was the best. He would even take the time to chop the vegetables up into tiny pieces so that we wouldn't choke on them. My grandfather put love into his food. I can smell that same kind of love in Susan's soup.

Although I don't live with my family anymore, my father still insists on making me soup and bringing it to me. Whether it's ox-tail, Ginseng, or vegetable soup, it tells me that he loves me. Don't ask me how I know—I can't explain it. The thing with Chinese elders is that they never say the words "I love you"—not in Chinese or English or any language. But they do say it in the way they cook their food.

But this chapter is not about soup or food. It is, however, about ingredients—the ingredients that have shaped Susan P.'s life as a Chinese person born and raised in Canada. When I interviewed Susan for this book in 2005, Susan's father was still living (he died in 2008) and was 96 years old. He arrived in Canada in 1921 at the age of 13. Like all Chinese immigrants during that time, he was required to pay the Head Tax. Susan isn't quite sure how much he paid.

"I think it was $50 or $500 those days," she says. "Those numbers ring a bell. But I do know he had documentation for it."

For decades, there was an ongoing joke about when Susan's father and the very few other Head Tax payers who were still alive would be reimbursed, or at least receive an apology from the federal government. I'm happy to say that Susan's father received compensation and an apology from the Canadian government in December 2006. It was long, long overdue.

Susan's father eventually had to travel back from Canada to China to marry, and Susan's older brother, Garry, was conceived there. But Susan's father couldn't bring his wife and son back to Canada due to the restrictive Canadian immigration laws at the time. Susan tells me that her mother was 40 years old before she was able to join her husband in Canada. The couple was separated for a total of somewhere between 10 and 15 years.

Upon his arrival in Vancouver some 80-odd years ago, we do know that he would have had to buy another identity — or "paper son" as they say — in order to get through all of the immigration restrictions of the day and settle down in one place. Susan's father went to Saskatoon, Saskatchewan, to work, but Susan can't recall the exact trail he took to reach his destination. Unlike most of the early Chinese immigrants who worked on the railroad, Susan's father worked in restaurants. After leaving Saskatoon and working in several small towns, he eventually settled in Edmonton.

Susan is first-generation Canadian-Chinese. She was born in Edmonton, Alberta, in the 1950s, a time when there were very few Chinese people in Edmonton. Susan and her sister were two of the few Chinese students in the grade school they attended. As the years went by, other Chinese families moved into the neighborhood, but Susan and her sister were still part of a visible minority in Edmonton, with the demographic landscape in the 1950s consisting mostly of Ukrainians and some First Nations, unlike the vast range of visible minorities we see today.

A Soup Called Love

"Was there a Chinatown back then?" I ask Susan.

"I don't recall much about that. I would think a store here and there, but not to the extent it is now. I do recall that if we needed Chinese goods, they would sometimes be exported from Vancouver. Of course I was quite young at that time. Much has changed."

When Susan was growing up, her mother was a stay-at-home mom, and her father was a waiter. Later, he would own his own restaurant. And that was the start of the delicious soup that Susan brings to work. A result of both love and hard work.

"When my dad was a waiter," Susan says, "he worked for other people. And he worked hard — extended hours in those days. I guess most immigrants' experience is 'work as much as possible.'"

As Susan speaks these words, I can tell she is very proud of her father and her mother. Her face lights up whenever she talks about her family.

One of the questions I ask Susan is whether it bothered her that her father didn't have an occupation similar to those of her Caucasian classmates' parents. But Susan doesn't think her father's occupations affected her or shaped her into the Chinese or Canadian person she is today.

"I don't think (it affected me)," she says. "And it was actually quite common. That's what people did in those days. Either you had your corner grocery store, you worked in a restaurant, or you owned your own restaurant. So I didn't think it was unusual—I thought it was normal. Everybody else you knew who was Chinese also worked in the same field. I don't think it had an impact on what I'm doing now or my outlook on the world. Other than, of course, that he worked hard."

So, for Susan, having a father who worked in a restaurant was just a part of life. Still, in spite of her acceptance of this, and the fact that she was very close to her family, Susan tells me she didn't want to be Chinese when she was young.

As with most Chinese immigrants struggling to survive in a new land, Susan's parents' expectations for her and her sister were high. These expectations included a good education and a desire for their children to take advantage of opportunities that they themselves never had. There were, however, differences between Susan's parents' attitudes as well.

"Dad probably wanted us to be more Canadian. More than Mom did. Mom is quite traditional, and she remains like that today. She celebrates all the holidays, as women do—they carry on that sort of business—and Dad, of course, was out in the working world. He's definitely more Canadian than Mom is."

I had expected that both parents would see things the same way—especially when it came to their culture. So I found these differences interesting. Susan's father just wanted to be Canadian and didn't believe in Chinese traditions, whereas her mother clung tightly to the Chinese ways. Her father spoke both English and Chinese, whereas her mother spoke only Chinese. In fact, when Susan's mother was given the opportunity to study English upon her arrival to Canada, she passed up the opportunity.

Despite her parent's differences in cultural outlooks, Susan's admiration for them is clearly evident.

"Your dad cooks really well," I say, and we both laugh.

"I'm very fortunate. Both of them are really good. When Dad was working, Mom was the cook. When dad retired, he sort of took over most times. But they work at it together now."

My compliments to the chefs!

Juggling the two languages was a struggle for Susan when she was growing up. She spoke only Chinese to her mother, and both English and Chinese to her father. So Susan spoke Chinese only at home — and only when necessary. Even now, she speaks only English to her husband, who is also Canadian-born Chinese. She also speaks English with her Chinese friends, except for the odd word that she can't translate.

"I lost a lot," she says.

"But do you still remember it when you speak to your parents now?"

"I struggle. It's a struggle because I didn't attend to my Chinese studies in those days." When Susan was young, she went to Chinese school for a while. "But not really," she says, "with the intention of studying. We just wanted to play."

This went on once a week when Susan was in grades one and two. Susan describes her time in Chinese school, which was held in a church basement:

"I remember sitting in desks, rows upon rows of them. I don't remember a lot, but I do remember we were taught to write the numbers. It is about all I remember. I wasn't too enthusiastic because you didn't want to be different in those days. You wanted to fit in with the others ... with the Caucasians, the whites ..."

The Chinese course was not part of the public school curriculum, where it is widely and successfully taught today. And, although many

Chinese students attended at the time Susan did, she had other plans after two years. She didn't want to study Chinese any further.

Not furthering her Chinese studies was Susan's way of rebelling. She believed it was the only way she could fit in. But she was also close to her family, and she was very accepting of her father not having a mainstream occupation. So why would she rebel? I would have expected the opposite to occur: that her being so close to her family would make her gravitate more toward her Chinese heritage. But it would seem that being close to one's family doesn't always play as huge of a role as I thought.

Susan's sister was two years younger than Susan, and they shared similar views. Susan's older brother, Garry, was almost out of the house by the time Susan was born. She and Garry are not close, but she assumes his views are more traditional than hers, since he was quite old when he immigrated and didn't attend grade school in Canada.

In terms of extended family, Susan didn't have much of one when she was growing up. For the most part, it was just her mother, her father, her sister, and herself. Susan's father did have one brother, but he passed away a long time ago. Her mother has a nephew whose son lives in Calgary, Alberta, but other than that, an extended family that might have helped reinforce the Chinese culture within Susan's life was all but non-existent.

Besides immediate family and extended family, other people of the same cultural background who live in the same neighborhood are also important in reinforcing a culture. In Susan's case, there were very few Chinese in Edmonton during the 1950s and 60s. Most of Susan's friends were Caucasians, although the closest ones were Chinese, few that they were. These Chinese friends shared the same culture and lived in the same neighbourhood as Susan. Overall, however, Susan felt equally comfortable with both groups when she was younger.

"I certainly felt I was in the minority, but I thought I was pretty secure in that. Of course, there was discrimination, and I did feel that as well. But I don't think I felt left out. Thinking back, I believed it was okay."

Although the Chinese community in Edmonton was small, Susan's parents did interact with other Chinese people during the early days. She talks about how the Chinese community came together:

"Other than church, they had their annual Chow Mein fundraiser event. They would sell tickets and everybody came. Even Caucasians came. It was quite open. I remembered Mom used to volunteer. All the ladies volunteered. I know they had this annually for quite awhile. And in the summer, the Chinese church held a picnic. That was also an annual thing for quite a number of years."

Unlike in her childhood, Susan isn't involved in any Chinese cultural events or associations now. The most she does is celebrate some aspects of the Chinese New Year.

"Pretty well nil on all that," she says. "I celebrate with Mom. She does celebrate with the different foods for Chinese New Year for example, and the burning of the incense. Offerings to the gods are generally what they do. But I don't participate in it. I just see my Mom doing it. Even when we were growing up she did it. But me—no—I don't have any direct associations with clubs or church."

When Susan was growing up, racism was displayed mostly in the form of name-calling. But she says she either brushed it off or avoided the source of the hatred. She was not a fighter. There were often incidents at school, but Susan figured there was no use in confronting the instigators—she figured it was their problem, not hers. Those people were simply not worthy of her or anybody's time.

Susan isn't sure of her parent's experiences with racism. If they did experience it, they never told her about it or discussed it with her. They just went on with their lives.

I ask Susan if she has any interest in going to China one day.

"No," she answers, "and I don't have any desire to go. I don't know why. I have seen videos and I have talked to people who have gone. I'm just not an adventurous traveller I guess."

What if someone gave her an all-expense paid ticket? Would she go then? She says she would, but not with great enthusiasm. There is no real pull there for her. And while she might go on an escorted tour, she maintains that she would never go alone. And even then, she says she might like to visit other parts of the Orient, but not necessarily China.

"How about visiting the village of your grandparents or your ancestors?" I ask. "Aren't you curious at least?" But, again, Susan expresses no real desire to visit these places—unless she just "happened to be in the area."

I ask Susan if she thinks that Edmonton has embraced more of the Chinese culture than it did 40 years ago.

"It has much improved since my days in grade school," she says. "I think ethnic groups are a valuable part of our community and the city, and our province."

"Like having a Chinese Lieutenant Governor (Norman Kwong)?" I ask.

"Yes. A fine example. Who would ever have thought? I think people have broader views now. People travel. There are so many different groups now, cultures, and religions, and they are all pretty well in the open."

Indeed, 200 years ago it was certainly unimaginable that a person of Chinese ancestry would represent the Queen in the Province of Alberta. Both Susan and I beam with pride.

Susan has a university degree and works within mainstream society. According to most theorists, the more highly educated you are and the more exposure you have to mainstream culture, the more likely you are to intermarry. Thus, I was certain that Susan's Chinese heritage would have little influence on her choice of husband. But I was wrong. She only ever dated Chinese men, and she married a Chinese man.

"During my dating years, I pretty well dated only Chinese guys. I didn't date non Chinese. I had good friends who weren't Chinese, but that was it. There was a cultural aspect to it, I guess. Or perhaps I considered my parents."

"Was it more for your parents' sake that you married Chinese or was it just simply the fact that your husband is a wonderful man?" I ask.

"Maybe it was the number of people I had acquainted myself with. They were probably mostly Chinese. Or maybe I did feel deeply attached to my cultural background. Maybe it was in the back of my mind. But it probably had more to do with just going with the flow and personal preference."

The pull between the two cultures was strong for Susan when she was growing up. Certain times of the year she couldn't do certain things because of the Chinese culture, such as not washing her hair during Chinese New Year because she would be washing away her good fortune. Another belief is that you aren't suppose to sweep or clean house during that day or time period or you will end up sweeping all your wealth out the door.

Susan talks about how traditional her mother was. "There are certain things you can eat, or shouldn't eat, when you're ill with something. If you have a fever, you shouldn't eat certain foods. If you have a cold sore, you shouldn't eat that. I'm generalizing, but that sort of thing. If you have a cold, then you should have this beverage or this concoction that Mom would make up."

"Because it's been handed down for thousands of years," I add.

"Yes. And if you had a bruise or a bump, Mom would have some sort of plaster to put on it to heal it. She would make a jar of gin and something like mud. It's very black and moist. Like a potion of some sort. There were certain things Mom always had on hand."

Susan's mother was an integral force in her life. It was from her that Susan gained, and learned about, Chinese culture and Chinese traditions. Since her mother was a housewife, Susan spent much more time with her than she did with her father. But the force of mainstream culture constantly pulled at her as well. In hindsight, Susan finds her struggle interesting. She no longer fights her feelings or struggles with them — she just goes with them.

Children, Susan points out, are always rebelling against something or someone because they don't have a good sense of the world yet or any real appreciation for what they have. And the tools to deal with different circumstances and situations haven't developed yet. Somehow, rebelling makes sense of the senseless. Now, as an adult, Susan has gained more of an understanding of the history of China and a deeper appreciation and respect for the Chinese culture.

"When I was younger, I didn't want to be different. I wanted to be like all the other Canadian kids. But I was different anyway, because there was so few of us. Now, though, I value the culture. I may not participate in it much, but I think it's great. I have another dimension to me as a non Caucasian person: things I'm aware of because of the way I grew up. And that combines with my Canadian side. So it sort of makes me more whole, whereas if you're just Canadian, you have only that aspect. It is richer when you have other parts of you. But I never considered that when I was a kid. I just didn't want to be different."

"So you're more comfortable in your own skin now?" I ask.

"Yes," she says. "I can think both ways. I feel much more comfortable."

Chinese Men Can Jump!

There is a 1992 movie called White Men Can't Jump, directed by Ron Shelton, and starring Woody Harrelson and Wesley Snipes. The movie centers on the stereotype that white men can't play basketball — or at least can't make a "slam dunk." Basketball hero Steve Nash would, however, beg to differ.

Naturally, many people would apply this same stereotype to Chinese men. But, in this case, it is Kevin Kwan — the "hero" of this chapter — who would beg to differ.

Kevin was born and raised in the small picturesque town of Smithers, British Columbia. Smithers is a beautiful, Swiss-themed town filled with mountains, lakes, and ski hills. It is, however, quite isolated. Vancouver is 12 hours away by car, and even the closest city to Smithers, Prince George, is a four-hour drive. Although Smithers is a "natural resource" kind of a town, full of miners, firefighters, foresters, and tree planters, it still tends to attract far more tourists than it does people who put down roots. Most people who happen by Smithers are either enjoying a ski vacation or are on their way to Alaska.

"It's the kind of place where you don't go by street names," Kevin tells me. "Instead it goes like this: 'Where are you going?' 'Oh, to so-and-so's house.' 'Okay. It's two blocks down past the pink house — the truck is parked outside — you can't miss it.'

"People just stop by one another's houses rather than calling ahead. I mean, there's no point in calling and asking, 'Are you home?' because everyone knows you're home. And everyone knows that that's so-and-so's uncle, who owns the butcher house or that's so-and-so's cousin."

This is the town that Kevin spent 17 years of his life in, before leaving to attend the University of Alberta in Edmonton. A town that had only six Asian families when Kevin lived there (besides the Kwans, there was one other Chinese family, a Vietnamese family, a Korean family, and two East Indian families) and even today has a population of only 6000 people.

So how did Kevin end up in Smithers? Well, let's start at the beginning.

Kevin's father was born in northeast China, in the Toishan area, in a village called Hoi Ping. He immigrated to Canada through his grandfather (Kevin's great grandfather), an early Chinese immigrant who worked on the Canadian railroad which ends in the Smithers area.

"He (Kevin's great grandfather) settled there afterwards," Kevin explains. "I believe he started a dry cleaning business way, way back. Then, when my great grandfather and my grandfather had saved enough money, they brought my dad over. My dad was thrown on a boat and came over to Canada with just the clothes on his back. He literally just showed up and started working with my great grandfather."

Kevin's father worked at whatever he could find to save up money. And with the money he saved, he and Kevin's grandfather bought an ice cream shop/restaurant, which eventually evolved into a Chinese restaurant.

Although Kevin's father went to grade school for only a few weeks upon his arrival to Canada, he was an entrepreneur at the core. And once he had established a thriving business, it was time to get married. So back to China he went to find a bride.

Kevin's mother was born in Canton, China, and later moved to, and grew up in, Hong Kong. The union of Kevin's parents was arranged by an aunt who lived in the same apartment building as Kevin's mother in Hong Kong.

When Kevin's father and mother returned to Canada, it didn't take long for most of their family members to follow.

"My mom had seven siblings, and my father had four," Kevin tells me. "And my dad was the only male in his family. In Asian households, that means you're the lead person whether you like it or not. My dad basically helped every one of my relatives immigrate—both his and hers (Kevin's mother), including my grandmother who lived with us and was the "queen," the head of the whole dynasty—over here and set them up all throughout Vancouver and northern BC."

Meanwhile, back in Smithers, Kevin's parents continued to run the Chinese restaurant and added to their repertoire a hotel, a liquor store, a nightclub, a daytime pub, and a number of other businesses all over town.

But Kevin's father's business acumen didn't begin and end with his own immediate family.

"He was kind of a like a franchise, if you will," Kevin tells me. "He set up every one of my aunts and uncles with a little restaurant, liquor store, hotel, or what-have-you. All the kids would laugh and call us the "Chinese Mafia," because every 30 miles or so there was another Chinese restaurant or hotel, and they were all owned by someone from our family.

"One good thing about it," Kevin continues, "is that if we ever had an out-of-town basketball game or something like that, we always knew we could eat at the Chinese restaurant and stay at the hotel for free, because we were family."

Kevin says the family businesses had an enormous influence on him as he was growing up. To some, the way his parents' ran their family life around their business might have been non traditional by North American standards, but it was stereotypically Chinese. And by stereotypical Chinese, it means a non mainstream occupation. As discussed earlier in the book, his parents would be in a mainstream occupation because of the high intensity of interaction with mainstream society.

"For me growing up," Kevin says, "this is where it gets a little weird. I never grew up in a house. We had a house — we had an acreage. But I lived at the restaurant with my mom and dad. They had rooms at the hotel, and I had a room there too. At the age of eight or ten, I'm doing dishes in the kitchen at the restaurant, helping out. I'm chopping vegetables for stir fries; I'm running food out to the smorgasbord table when it's empty. Sometimes I'm outside cleaning tables or bussing tables. At 14, I'm selling liquor at our liquor store to help out or working the service line, where people can't see me, at the nightclub. At 15, I'm watching my brothers throw drunks out of the club."

"So, I guess when you look at it, it wasn't a very traditional way of growing up — not in any facet."

Indeed!

I ask Kevin what his parents' ideals were as far as raising their children. His answer can, perhaps, be summed up in one word: "liberal."

"My parents weren't that involved in our growing up," Kevin says. "A: They had never been in school themselves, so they didn't really know what it was—they just knew we should be in it. And B: They never grew up with that much structure in their own families. There was no 'it's 5 o'clock, time to eat' — they were always working. So we were just kind of left to take care of ourselves. I mean, it's not like we had to fend for ourselves against the whole world, but it was like, 'if you want to join the basketball team, okay… I don't know what that is, but whatever.' Of course, this isn't to say that they didn't care. It was just the way they did things. And my oldest sibling is my sister—she was actually more like our mother. She would go to school and do the parent-teacher thing because my mom had no clue what that was."

Kevin says he became particularly aware of the peculiarities in his family when he saw how other families in Smithers lived and interacted. Then he noticed that there was a huge difference between his Chinese family and the Caucasian families of his peers.

"For us," Kevin says, "we had a restaurant. So we just showed up and ate whenever we wanted to. We had a family dinner maybe once a year at Christmas. But usually what would happen is that we would show up at home, and my dad and mom would both be working. My brother and I might say, 'I'm hungry,' and Mom might make something, put it on the table in the back room of the kitchen, and go right back to work. And we would eat quickly, and then go to, say, basketball practice or go play video games, or whatever. Later on, my sister would show up, and she would eat and do her thing. It was pretty much like a gas station—you just showed up for food when you needed it."

All of those differences aside, did Kevin feel like he fit in with the other kids in town? Not really, he tells me.

"I'm six feet tall," Kevin points out, "and that's pretty tall for an Asian person. But, still, when I was a kid, everyone I hung out with was a lot taller than me. So whether it was height or race, I was still the minority in the group. I would go to a house party with friends and everyone would talk to the Caucasian people and the Asian person was just ... well ... seen as different. At first I thought it was just me, but then I realized that I'm a pretty social person. If, for instance, I'm in a setting where there are a lot of Asian people, I'm very social. But it was different then—I don't know if people were intimidated or if I was really that different or what.

"There's a lot of different aspects to 'fitting in' though. We could be talking about everything from what you take to school for lunch to what you do with your free time. And, for me, sometimes it was about money. I was able to do pretty much everything, because my parents would happily pay for it. If I told my mom that something cost a hundred dollars, she would just give it to me. That's Asian culture—it says 'let's just provide, make sure they're getting the experience.' But then other kids would see me as being spoiled—they would make sure to point out that they had to pay for these things themselves, or had to do chores, or whatever. But they didn't realize how much work I actually did, how much I helped out with the family businesses—carrying luggage, shoveling snow, stocking liquor, washing dishes—whatever. They just assumed I was a rich kid who got everything for nothing."

Another assumption Kevin struggled against was the stereotypical idea that Asians aren't good at sports. As a result, Kevin often second guessed himself when it came to the activities he participated in.

"You're Asian," he explains, "you shouldn't be good at sports, you should be good at math. You shouldn't be playing sports; you should be playing piano. But I grew up the exact opposite. None of our family did those traditional arts and culture things. We were jocks."

Kevin then tells me, in a hushed tone, that people have actually told him that he's pretty good at sports ... for an Asian guy. I laugh — why shouldn't he be? Does being Asian mean he can't jump? Kevin tells me that not only did he play sports, but he also coached, volunteered, and taught classes. How very unAsian of him!

We talk a little more about Kevin's experience as a young student, and he tells me that when he was going to school all the visible minorities hung out in their own segregated groups. Whether this was because they shared the same challenges or because they were equally discriminated against, Kevin isn't sure. Kevin himself hung out with a group composed of East Indian kids and other Asian kids. There was also a First Nations group and a Caucasian group (the Caucasian group being, of course, the largest). There was, Kevin tells me, a definite pecking order. The Caucasians picked on the First Nations, and the First Nations picked on the other visible minorities. Fortunately, the kids being picked on defended themselves with punches rather than guns and knives.

Kevin also points out that he was lucky in that he came from a large family and had lots of brothers who always looked out for one another.

But even with that brotherly protection, Kevin still often felt like a walking target. And it wasn't always other kids who gave him grief.

"We also got it," Kevin says, "from our teachers. Not all of them, but some of them for sure. They just didn't have any respect for the Asian way, and they often resented our prosperity. For instance, there was this one math teacher who was giving all the students this big long lecture about how math is so important, and you need it to get into a good university or get a good job, or whatever. And that's fine — that's a message you would expect to hear from a math teacher. But then he said, 'Unless, of course, your family owns a restaurant. Then you can just buy your way into university.' It was pretty obvious that he was directing that comment toward my family. And he said it right in front of everyone."

Given all of the challenges Kevin faced, I ask how he fared academically.

"Did we do well in school?" Kevin shrugs. "We did okay — but we didn't really put a lot of time or effort into it. Our parents didn't know anything about school, so they never told us to study or do our homework when we got home. So we just kind of did what we wanted, and that was usually playing sports, playing video games, hanging out with friends … but I'm happy for that. I wouldn't have done it any other way. I look at it now, and I realize that I'm the kind of person who likes to do a little bit of everything. For me to spend five extra hours studying … would I have gotten better marks? Sure. But I would have missed out on a lot of other stuff. I did enough (academically) to get into post-secondary, and now I have a wealth of experiences and skills to fall back on, as opposed to just one or two."

Discrimination was a constant theme in Kevin's childhood — not only for him personally, but for his entire family. Perhaps the only person who escaped overt discrimination was his mother, but that, Kevin says, is because she was always in the back of the restaurant working and had very little interaction with members of the community.

"We didn't fit in at all," Kevin tells me. "One of us would be walking down the street and old men we didn't even know would start verbally abusing us and accusing us of doing things we didn't do. And I couldn't count on a calculator the number of times I would be walking home from elementary school and someone would ride by on their bike and call me 'Chink.'

"The one story that really sticks out in my mind came from my father. There's a reason he quit school. He did go for two or three weeks, but he was discriminated against so badly — both physically and verbally — that he just quit."

"This was in Smithers?" I ask.

"Yes, in Smithers. He told me that one day after school, he got into an altercation after school because some kids were picking on him. He got so frustrated and worried that he grabbed a chair and defended himself. There's a lot of resentment when you grow up that way. I remember the first fight I got into. I got beat up by some kid, and I had no idea what to do. I went home knowing my dad would find out because, for one, my brothers would tell him, and for the other, I had a black eye.

"The first words out of my dad's mouth, even before he knew exactly what the situation was, were, 'You don't let those f...ing kids bug you. If you have to take a chair and defend yourself with it, you do it!' So I'm sitting there thinking, 'What do you do?'"

Outside of school, because of his involvement in sports, Kevin often hung out more with Caucasian kids than he did with minority kids. But he still always felt more comfortable in his Asian friends' homes than he did in his Caucasian friends' homes.

"You go to the Caucasian friend's house for dinner," Kevin tells me, "and everybody's sitting at the table, and everybody's got a place setting. It's very much like what you see on TV. And my family never did that. It was a novelty and a treat at first, but then I would stick out even more. My friend's parents would ask me, 'Oh, are your mom and dad coming to the basketball game?' and what do I say? 'No. They're working, and they don't even know that I play?' That makes it sound like they don't care — but it's not that; it's just that it's not a priority. But the other parents would just think, 'Oh — well that's weird.'"

Inviting friends over to his house for supper was also a challenge for Kevin.

"Sometimes I would bring my friends home for dinner," he says, "but 'dinner' in our house meant that we would go to the back of the kitchen and eat something from the restaurant. They were usually nice about it, but you could tell they thought it was strange. And all of sudden you would feel really small because you felt so different. Eventually, I just figured out there were certain things I shouldn't say, or information I shouldn't share, because people would always look at me funny when I did."

Kevin also faced subtle forms of discrimination when he played sports in other communities. He tells me that people would look at him as if they expected him to ask them to repeat the instructions—as if he didn't speak English.

And then there was the matter of money—yet one more reason to ostracize Kevin and his family.

"People just assumed we were wealthy," Kevin says, " I remember my brothers and me trying to apply for university scholarships through the school. There were Caucasian families that were far wealthier than us—we were pretty much middle class. But we were told directly that we shouldn't bother applying because we were too wealthy. Yet there were kids whose families were far wealthier than ours who were applying for them and getting them."

But, Kevin says, it wasn't all bad. In spite of the discrimination, Kevin claims that a lot of good also came out of his childhood in Smithers. He points in particular to watching how hard his mother worked and how kind she was to everyone.

"She would spend 30 minutes talking to customers," he says, "even if they were there for a twenty-five cent cup of coffee. She would teach them a Chinese word or two. And if a customer couldn't pay, she would tell them not to worry about it, they could pay next time.

"And she made all of her dishes from scratch—like her chicken soup, which she sold for two dollars a bowl. Sure, she could have warmed up something processed, but that just wasn't her style."

Kevin also concedes that for all the people who picked on him, there were also some really great people in Smithers. In particular, his track coach.

"My track coach," Kevin says, "was one of my biggest mentors. He got every ounce of performance out of us, regardless of who we were or what gender, age, or race we were. He always treated everyone with the utmost respect. He was one of the best coaches in this country, bar none, and I've seen a lot of coaches in my time. He was someone who could make people achieve to one hundred percent of their ability, even if they weren't natural athletes."

There was also another Chinese family in Smithers—Kevin's grandmother's best friend's family. This family also ran a Chinese restaurant in town. And all of the children (three boys and one girl) were close in age to the Kwan children (five boys and one girl). All of the children, Kevin tells me, practically grew up together—the two families were almost like one big family. Everyone spoke Chinese, and everyone shared similar experiences, whether those experiences had to do with working in the family businesses or with being a part of a visible minority in a small town.

Family, in general, had a huge presence in Kevin's childhood. Because Smithers was the largest community of the small British Columbia towns that Kevin's extended family lived in, it became the natural gathering point. On Thursday, Friday, or Saturday nights, Kevin tells me, all the relatives would get together in Smithers and play mahjong, watch TV, or simply visit. And all of his relatives, including those who were living in Vancouver at the time, would gather to celebrate Chinese New Years together. Kevin credits his knowledge of the Chinese culture to these gatherings.

"We learned about the culture just by seeing it," he says. "We saw, for instance, how my grandmother paid respect to people who had passed away. And we learned about food. My grandmother had a garden on our acreage, and she grew all Chinese vegetables—bok choy and things like that. No typical carrots and potatoes. And our family often had traditional food shipped in from Vancouver—or we picked it up—things like barbeque duck, for instance. And we made a lot of the traditional foods ourselves as well."

Kevin and his siblings were also fortunate enough to be able to go to Vancouver to visit relatives on a fairly regular basis, particularly in the summer. Although the Kwan family may not have been as wealthy as the other residents of Smithers thought they were, they were prosperous enough that the entire family could fly to Vancouver for a weekend. In Vancouver, Kevin encountered even more opportunities to participate in the Chinese culture.

Family was also the reason Kevin was able to maintain his Chinese language. (He and his siblings, of course, never went to Chinese school because Smithers didn't have one.)

"The reason we learned Chinese at all," Kevin tells me, "is that my grandmother never spoke any English, and she was living with us. My mom also speaks very little English. So we always talked to them and to my aunts and uncles in Chinese."

Kevin tells me that his father does speak mostly English, but he also spoke Chinese to Kevin's mother, grandmother, and aunts and uncles.

"They encouraged us to speak Chinese because we had to," Kevin says. "And they showed us how to properly do prayers for our relatives who have passed away. My mother was always teaching us little things, like, 'this is why we do this—this is the reason for this ceremony.' And other people would tell us, 'You need to do this.'"

Kevin still tries to maintain his Chinese language. And he's comfortable with how much he knows—enough, he says, to get by in Hong Kong or China.

"I practice it when I go to eat at restaurants," he tells me. "And some friends and I will speak Chinese to one another just for fun—although we usually speak English because it feels a bit weird to speak Chinese to someone you've spoken English to from the first time you met them. And I still practice my Chinese when I visit my aunts and uncles."

"What about with your siblings?" I ask.

"All English," he says, "unless we're making fun. We do it sometimes when we're on the volleyball or basketball court. We can say signals and say what we're suppose to do without people understanding our plays. Little things like that."

Kevin goes on to tell me that, even for all of his knowledge of Chinese culture, he really only notices its influence in his life when he stops to compare it to North American culture. For instance, he says, to him it wasn't a big deal that his grandmother lived with them, but there are many who would be uncomfortable with that arrangement. Still, Kevin maintains that the things that influence him are the things his parents taught him, rather than him putting any thought into what Chinese culture is "supposed" to be.

Kevin has also been to China—twice. The first time he went, as a youngster, it was with his father and his brother, Rick. Their father showed the boys the house where he grew up, and they visited relatives—some of Kevin's great uncles and aunts, from both his mother's and his father's sides of the family, still live there. Some live in poverty and some are well off. Some are government officials, some are in the police force, some are farmers who want to stay on their farms, and some are entrepreneurs.

"It was really an eye opener for me," Kevin tells me. "I definitely appreciated it—and it sparked more interest in the Asian culture. When

I have kids, I definitely want them to have that same experience because it's something you just can't understand until you're immersed in it. You get there and you think, 'Wow, there might be other people in the world who appreciate the same things I appreciate.' I participated in the rural customs—I even ate dog."

At this point I just have to ask, "What does dog taste like?"

"It doesn't really taste that different," Kevin says, "It was just a little more tough version of beef."

"Does it have a smell?" (I just can't contain my curiosity!)

"No, not really. Anyway," Kevin says, determined to move on. "The point is that I've had those experiences—I saw how there's no electricity and how everyone rode bikes. In some respects, it really made me appreciate how I grew up. But at the same time, I think I wish I had more of those same values that I saw over there."

The second time Kevin went to China was in 1999, and he was once again accompanied by his brother Rick. This time, the two of them were there on an exchange trip. They, along with 1,200 other Chinese students from around the world, spent two months living there. Kevin tells me that this particular exchange trip was a political move on the part of the Taiwanese government, which was hoping to convince the western world to support its bid for independence from China. In order to participate in the exchange program, the students had to be of Chinese descent, from relatively affluent families, and enrolled in university. The Taiwanese government wined and dined the students, but the students also took classes in culture, art, and cooking while they were there. Kevin says he knew he was part of a political ploy, but it didn't really bother him.

"We felt comfortable," he says. "All of a sudden we wanted to embrace the Asian culture even more because we didn't see it as being either on this side or that side. Instead, we thought, '"Wow. There's so many different ways that we can be part of the North American culture and still have our Asian culture as well."'

This is not to say, however, that Kevin always felt like he "fit in" or that he automatically belonged.

"It was a fantastic experience," he tells me. "We saw everything from the rural settings where 20 people lived on one farm with no electricity to the urban settings of Hong Kong and Beijing. But I have to admit that I still didn't feel quite like I totally fit in anywhere. There were times that Rick and I might as well have been Caucasian, we were so out of place. People would sometimes stare at us just as if we were foreigners. Part of it was because we were a lot taller than most of the people there, and we were different in other ways too. For one thing, we couldn't handle the humidity, and we would just walk around sweating all the time. Or maybe it was the language, or the way we dressed, or whatever."

So, while Kevin is intimately aware of his Chinese culture, this also led to some confusion on his part.

"I didn't really know what I wanted a lot of the time," he says. "And mostly it wasn't that I was choosing one culture over the other. It was more that I was looking at what I thought was right or wrong and what I grew up with."

More often than not, Kevin says, he did what his parents told him to do. And he was often left without a lot of guidance or structure. He wasn't always sure what was Chinese and what wasn't, what was Buddhist and what wasn't, or, as he says, "what came from a cereal box." He just wasn't always sure of where he came from or why he did what he did—other than that he was told to do them.

"Ever heard of the saying, 'Children should be seen but not heard?'" he asks me. "That's a pretty predominant belief in the Chinese culture."

Kevin tells me that he still struggles with some of the questions he has around his Chinese identity.

"Some of the confusion is still there," he says. "But now it's more of a question of which path I want to go down. I'm not going to worry about or make up for the past or what I did or didn't get. Now it's more a matter of where I want to go from here. Do I want to go the route of learning more about my culture? Do I want to go the route of finding a wife, having kids, and immersing them into that culture?"

Kevin is also quick to point out that, while he did, for the most part, do what he was told, he also had his moments of rebellion.

"I remember," he says, "that my dad was very upset with me one time because I went and washed dishes at another restaurant. I had decided I would rather work somewhere else, somewhere with a little more structure, so I could experience something different. But my dad never understood why I did it. I tried to tell him that it wasn't about the money, and it wasn't about not wanting to help my parents out — in fact, I told him that I would still be helping out at home. But I wanted to do something different too. And I just wanted to be like everyone else — some of my friends would be working here or there, ¬¬a restaurant, a ski hill, a lodge, and I wanted to have the same experiences as them. I wanted to be able to talk with my friends about our boss or other people we worked with, or trade shifts with them, or whatever. And I was missing out on those things. But I couldn't get my dad to understand that."

Kevin's biggest point of rebellion, however, came when he graduated from high school, and his father declared that he (Kevin) would study in the Business program at the University of British Columbia, just as his brother had. But Kevin had different plans. He wanted to enroll in the Physical Education program at the University of Alberta. This signified, of course, a very non traditional career path within the Chinese culture. And Kevin's father didn't take kindly to the idea. In fact, he said, "NO WAY!"

But Kevin had his own way of getting the ball in the hoop. He simply made sure that he didn't get accepted into any of the programs that his father preferred. Besides applying to the Physical Education program at the University of Alberta, Kevin also studiously applied for acceptance into Master's programs at the University of Victoria and Simon Fraser University and an Honors program at the University of British Columbia. Of course, as most people know, you are required to have a Bachelor's degree before you can apply for acceptance into a Master's program. And Kevin, who had only a high school diploma, was well aware of this. His father, however, wasn't. When all was said and done, Kevin gathered together all of his rejection letters from these various institutions and showed them to his father. And then Kevin pulled out the one acceptance letter he had received—from the University of Alberta. The message was clear: Kevin would either take Physical Education at the University of Alberta or he would simply stay home. Fortunately, Kevin's father agreed that it was better to take any program than to take none at all. And so Kevin left Smithers and made his way to Edmonton. While Kevin was attending the University of Alberta, he had the opportunity to run track and was offered a scholarship. He also played volleyball. Just as Kevin had suspected, the Physical Education program turned out to be the perfect fit for him. And, although the sports were the clincher, there were a lot of other little things that drew Kevin to Edmonton and, ultimately, contributed to his decision to make it his permanent home.

"I basically moved here for a couple of reasons," he tells me. "I also wanted to get away from my family. My brothers all went to school in Vancouver, and they all lived the traditional 'live at home, grandmother cooks all the meals' kind of a life. Sort of your more typical Asian progression of events. But I wanted to go somewhere

where I would be on my own, pay my own bills, cook my own meals, live my own life. And just be 'me' instead of the brother of so-and-so.

"And Edmonton still has a small town feel. Vancouver is too cliquey. Everybody there always seems to me to be too concerned with what they're wearing—or what other people are wearing. Or what your parents did for a living or what kind of car you drive. And I'm just not like that—I'm more of a 'get to know the person before making any judgments' kind of a person."

It's pretty clear that Kevin had a rather unique experience growing up, and I can't help but wonder if all of the Kwan children had similar experiences. Kevin tells me that this isn't the case—particularly for the older children. And these different childhoods also produced different results.

Kevin's oldest brother Mike and his oldest sister Grace didn't go to university at all, for example. And Mike is very, in Kevin's words, "anti-Chinese."

"We (the other siblings)," Kevin tells me, "often joke that he's a Chinese redneck. He sings country music, and only country music, in karaoke bars. He's a mechanic and a welder. He builds monster trucks and muscle cars, and he's a mudbog racer."

Mike also speaks Chinese very sparingly—and only to his mother. And he doesn't really care to know much about the Chinese culture. This, Kevin tells me, is true of most of the older children in the family. Doug, who is the next in line after Grace and Mike, was the first to move to Vancouver to attend university, but he also cares little about the Chinese culture. Dave, the next oldest, is somewhat interested in the culture, Kevin tells me, but only because of the food. "He's always wanting to know where the best Chinese restaurant is," Kevin laughs. In general, Rick (who is older than Kevin by 11 months) and Kevin have the strongest ties to the Chinese culture. But, Kevin points out, they also had very different experiences and opportunities than the older ones.

"There's an age gap of 14 years between Mike and I," Kevin says. "When Mike was in high school, I was just a baby. And there were probably even fewer visible minorities around then, so the older kids were probably much more susceptible to discrimination and more pressured to fit in. Now they just want to assimilate and don't have much interest in Chinese culture beyond having the language."

Also, Kevin tells me, of all the siblings who spent time in the city (whether Vancouver or Edmonton), only he and Rick ever really embraced the city life.

"For Rick and I," he explains, "it was a different experience than it was for the older ones. They were less social than Rick and I, so they just kind of kept their friends from high school, who were all Caucasian. But Rick and I started making all kinds of friends—Asian friends—right away. And, for me anyway, it was great to all of a sudden have 30 new friends who were both Asian like me and Canadian like me. When we would have get togethers, if my mom was there, my female friends would know to greet her as "auntie" (a respectful acknowledgement to a female Chinese elder). It was so comforting in a way—everyone in the room understood the Chinese culture, and no one looked at me like I was weird."

But not all of his friends now are Asian, Kevin tells me. "Some of my best friends are Caucasian. And they're the most liberal and open-minded people—people who set fine examples in their communities. Teachers, doctors, volunteers. And they all have a sense of fairness, equality, and tolerance."

But it's not like life in Edmonton has been perfect for Kevin. Discrimination is discrimination, regardless of whether it happens in a small town or a big city.

"I've been pulled over so many times by the police and had my car searched," Kevin says, "when all I'm doing is driving back from playing volleyball at 11 p.m. And I've been told by friends in the police force that they do target the Asian population because that gives them a higher chance of finding what they're looking for — drug dealers and the such. Fair enough. But from my perspective, I find it interesting how many times that's happened to me in comparison to a Caucasian person, and I wonder what happens to other Asian kids in the city. It's almost like you can't avoid it — no matter how innocent you are. You just fall into a certain category and that's that."

Kevin shares another unforgettable experience he had in the city when he was in his early twenties.

"Rick and I were walking up to the line-up to get into a nightclub," he says. "We got to the front door and the doorman turned to us and said, literally, 'Sorry, we're not allowing ethnics in here tonight. You guys caused too much trouble here last week, so this week we're not letting you in.' There was a policeman standing at the door, and we got into an argument with him, and he threatened to arrest us. I was so upset — I mean, I can understand a private establishment having the right to refuse entry. But you shouldn't be able to tell me that I'm not allowed in because I'm 'ethnic.' Or have a city police officer in full uniform, being paid by my tax dollars, enforcing a human rights violation."

Kevin tells me that this experience continued to eat at him long after it was over. Fortunately, he says, the principal (who happened to be a woman of African descent) of the culturally diverse school at which he was working at the time helped him put things into perspective.

"She said to me, 'Kevin, you're an educated man. You're polished and professional. You volunteer in the community and so many people respect you. You're an upstanding person. Some of the kids you work with dress like gang bangers and have criminal records. They get discriminated against all the time — who's going to listen to them or believe what they say? You're in a position to say something and have people listen. So do you think maybe you should be looking at this as an opportunity to represent the people of your culture?'

"I looked and her," Kevin concludes, "and said, 'you're absolutely right.'"

That conversation had an incredible impact on Kevin, and he says that he now tries to concentrate more on showing people, through his actions, that their preconceived notions are wrong as opposed to seeking out personal "justice."

Kevin has come a long way since his days growing up in Smithers. I ask him if he would ever consider moving back there.

"It's a place to visit, but not to live," he shrugs. "If I ever did go back, it would depend on what stage of my life I was in, considering that I have a university degree and considering the types of jobs and industries that Smithers has to offer. Maybe later on when I have a family I'll start thinking about the cleaner air and the access to lakes and decide to move back. But then I'd also lose a lot of amenities — like access to Chinese schools for my kids and being able to go to live hockey games."

And now that he lives in the city, Kevin looks back at the difficulties of his childhood as blessings in disguise. If, for instance, he's in a nightclub with friends, he is able to spot trouble coming "from a mile away," because he became so accustomed to seeing it when he was a child. Now, he says, he can just tell his friends that something's about to happen, and they avoid it by leaving. He knows how to mix drinks, how to cook, how to manage money, and how to run a business all because of his childhood experiences.

Kevin had to grow up really fast, he says. He had to become an adult whether he wanted to or not. "I had a lot of 'adult' experiences when I was a kid," he says. "I saw people get arrested in our clubs. I saw people start fights and get injured. I saw people come in and spend money that should have been for groceries on booze."

But Kevin also developed a strong work ethic, based on the example his parents set.

"Now," he says, "I do whatever it takes to get a job done. When I was 13, every Thursday evening, I would have to unload pallets of beer, wine, and liquor by hand for the liquor store. I mean, a big semi truck shows up—what do you do? You unload the beer. Now, I sometimes clean exercise equipment (Kevin is the president of Kwantum Wellness Centre in downtown Edmonton), and people ask me why I'm doing it. Well, usually it's because whoever was supposed to do it didn't show up, but someone has to do it. Why not me? I grew up doing whatever jobs needed to be done, so it doesn't bother me. When I was a kid, when my parents' hired staff wouldn't show up, I would have to forgo my Friday night plans to wash dishes. I don't want the people who work for me to have to do that."

Kevin does admit, however, that he can be a bit obsessive at times. If a job description says to do something, he generally tries to do two or three times more than what is called for. He's always trying to take things "just a couple of notches higher." He's not at all apologetic about that, though.

"You shape your attitude that way. I guess my attitude is "get it done the best way possible and in the most realistic way possible. Which doesn't necessarily mean that it's perfect. You do have to compromise a bit if you need to get ten things done. But you can't hire someone to do just one thing just because you don't want to do it yourself."

I ask Kevin if he thinks his occupation has any influence on how he identifies with the Chinese culture. He says it doesn't—to him, work is work and culture is culture. Perhaps if he was in a more culture-related business, he says, it would have more influence. But, generally, he doesn't believe it has much influence on whether he does, or doesn't, maintain his culture. He does say, however, that it really bothers him when he encounters some of the stereotypes around this topic (i.e. shouldn't he be running a Chinese restaurant, or be a doctor, or something more typically "Chinese?").

From the subject of work, we turn to the subject of marriage. Kevin tells me that only one of his brothers, Doug, is married — to a Caucasian girl.

"She's a great person," Kevin says, "and she's been accepted into the family. Mom would prefer for us to marry Chinese women, but, really, it's up to us. There hasn't been any friction in the family or anything like that. But there are some challenges."

As examples of these challenges, Kevin points to the fact that Chinese people eat certain Chinese foods in certain ways — ways that his sister-in-law doesn't understand and struggles with. And the family often makes fun of Kevin's mom's soup, which, according to her, can increase hair growth or make you jump higher. For Chinese people, it's pretty common to hear such claims, but non Chinese people often don't "get it" and end up feeling left out of the joke. And then there's the matter of passing down recipes: Kevin's mother has given him many of her recipes for traditional Chinese foods because he loves to cook, but she struggles to communicate those same recipes to her daughter-in-law.

Kevin's brother Doug and his wife have three boys. The boys don't speak Chinese nor are they in Chinese school.

"My mom goes to see them," Kevin says, "and it's hard, because she can't really communicate with them because she doesn't speak much English."

Kevin is quick to point out that that's not a result just of his sister-in-law being Caucasian. "Part of it is also that my brother is more assimilated into the North American culture and doesn't really pursue anything Chinese," he says.

This also presents a challenge to Kevin's extended family. His cousins all married Chinese people, and they all put their children in Chinese schools. And, Kevin says, the connections between family members remain as strong as they were when Kevin was growing up.

"But," Kevin says, "I see my nephews not having that same connection with all of our relatives. It's almost like they're cut off from having any kind of influence from the Asian side. She (Kevin's sister-in-law) knows a few Asian words here and there, but there's only so far you can go to make up for that. And it's not any fault of hers—it's just that there are certain consequences that come with marrying outside the culture."

Kevin doubts that his nephews will ever research their Chinese culture, especially once their grandmother is gone. But he hopes that they will—Kevin and his siblings are first-generation Canadians, and Kevin would like to believe that his generation won't be the last generation of the Kwan family to speak Chinese and reinforce the Chinese culture.

"That's the power of language," Kevin says. "You can add 70 more members to a group if you all speak the same language, but you can lose 40 if you don't."

Kevin is quick to point out, however, the many ways in which his sister-in-law enriches all of their lives and how a willingness to give and take can benefit everyone. "She teaches me how to make stuffing for Thanksgiving," he says, "and in return, I teach her how to make wonton soup."

Kevin tells me he believes that while his culture will affect his choice of a significant other, it's certainly not the only factor. That is, he wouldn't date or marry a woman just because she's Chinese. He just wants someone he can connect with, and if she's Chinese, that's a bonus as far as he's concerned because it would make it easier for him to maintain his culture and to pass it on to his children. Still, he says he wouldn't take it so far as to make it a condition. Yes, he would like to put his children in Chinese school, and should he marry a woman who isn't Chinese, he figures it's something he and his wife would decide together. And while he does want to pass his culture on to his children, he also doesn't want to "force" it on them.

So how is Kevin directly involved in the Chinese culture now? He is president of the Edmonton Dragon Boat Race Club, which is definitely Asian influenced, and he used to teach morning exercises to Chinese seniors. He also loves to try out different Chinese restaurants, both because he loves the food and because it gives him a chance to practice his Chinese. He keeps in touch with a lot of the Chinese kids he used to teach, and they keep him up to date with the "pop culture" side of Chinese/Asian things. Listening to Chinese music is also a part of his life. And, of course, he still speaks Chinese to his family.

I ask Kevin if there are parts of the Chinese culture that he identifies more, or less, strongly with.

"I can identify with all of it," he tells me, "but I don't necessarily agree with all of it. For one thing, I don't agree with the tendency to think only about money. I can understand that one needs to be financially sound, but a lot of the Chinese traditions are, well, it's like, 'How much money do you make?' or 'You have to find a husband or wife who makes a lot of money.' And a lot of Chinese believe that the fatter you are, the more prosperous you are. The 'faat daat' ('wealthy' in Chinese). I don't agree with that at all—I'm more into personal health. I also don't agree with the idea that Asian wives should be subservient and do all the cooking and cleaning.

"But what I'm totally for are the family connections. I like the idea of having people to babysit, watch the kids, do things with. I don't mind the idea of three generations—grandparents, parents, children—all living in one house. I see a huge advantage to those types of Chinese traditions."

I ask Kevin if he's more proud of being Canadian or of being Chinese. He thinks he's equally proud of both. When he was young, he says, he was less proud to be Chinese. It's not that he didn't acknowledge it then, but he was less public, less sure, about it. Now, he says, he's older, more confident, and more proud of his heritage. He tells me that when he watches the Olympics, he is proud to be Canadian, and he roots for China as well. If anything, he says, his struggle is not with one or the other, but with combining the two.

"I like dim sum," he says, "and I like bacon and eggs. I enjoy both of the cultures — and I notice and appreciate the differences between them. But sometimes you can't have them both because they clash. And then I think, 'Which one do I want more?' or 'Is it easier for me to just do what everyone else is doing or what my family is doing?' So, it's sort of 50-50 a lot of the time — half Chinese, half Canadian. And there are many times I wish that both could work together all the time."

No, really, where are you from? I ask Kevin if he has been asked this question, and he tells me that he has — many times.

"I tell people I'm from Smithers," he says. "And they say, 'Where's that?' and I say 'Smithers, British Columbia.' And they say, 'No really, where are you from?'

"I just try to explain, patiently, that you can be born in Winnipeg and be of Italian ancestry, or born in New York and of African ancestry."

And then Kevin hits the nail on the head.

"The problem," he says, "is that people aren't asking what they actually mean to ask. What they actually mean to ask (and maybe think they're asking) is what your cultural background is. But they don't seem to realize that that's something different, all together, than where you're from."

For his part, Kevin just asks the "real" question when he talks to people. "I have lots of Caucasian friends, and if I want to know what their cultural background is, I just ask them—I don't ask them where they're from, unless, of course, that's actually what I want to know.

"And," Kevin continues, "I'm not sure why people are so afraid of asking that question or why they feel they have to do a song and dance to get at the information they want. I'm never afraid to ask—it's not taboo, it's not a sensitive subject, and it's not going to offend anyone, so what's the big deal?"

Kevin shares another experience:

"I met a friend of a friend, and he says, 'Are you Chinese?' And to me that's progress, straight up. So I say, 'Yeah.' But then he says to me, 'I know this great Chinese restaurant in such-and-such a place, have you ever been there?' I was kind of baffled and speechless. And I wondered what he would think if I said, 'What do you think of the hot dogs at such-and-such a place?'"

Both of us laugh, and I tell Kevin how I once had some Caucasian people, none of whom I knew, attempt to speak Chinese to me, as if they thought that if I nodded my head enough times to indicate that I understood, we would eventually have this fluid, lively, genuine Chinese conversation.

And then there is the standard "Oh, I have a friend who is Chinese—do you know him?" question.

At this point, Kevin reminds me that these incidents are rarely the result of any malicious intent—rather, they're the result of simple ignorance. And Kevin believes that Chinese people themselves have a critical role to play in clearing up that ignorance.

"If we, as Chinese descendants," Kevin says," are going to make our culture stand on its own two feet, we have to encourage diversity ourselves. If we do nothing but follow the stereotypes—if we do nothing but open restaurants—that's all we're going to be known for. And I'm not saying that restaurants are bad or that no Chinese person should ever open one again. I'm just saying we need more diversity.

Everybody wants diversity—everybody wants something challenging to do. And our culture should be the same."

There's a whole lot more to the Chinese culture than the steaming restaurant or the gang member standing on the corner waiting for the next hit. We can go—and do go—so much further. And as much as other aspects of our lives (business or marriage) require challenges and variety, so does our culture.

"We shouldn't lose our culture, but we should embrace other things as well—diversify what we do. We should do more than just the things that Chinese people have done for centuries. We should carry some of those traditions on, yes, but we should also be changing what doesn't make sense and doing so much more. And then no one could ever say, 'All Chinese people are like this, or like that, or do this, or do that,' just like they don't ever paint all Caucasian people with the same brush."

And, with that, our interview draws to a close. And I have to admit that I'm impressed by Kevin. I think he's a great role model for young Chinese men who often face so much pressure: pressure from friends who glamorize the gang and drug lifestyles and from parents who expect so much and turn education or work into a competition to see who can get the best marks or make the most money.

It's difficult, I think, for young Chinese people today to find mentors or role models they can relate to from their own cultural background, who are not rehabbed rap singers or scantily clad celebrities. It's hard for them to find someone real, someone like Kevin Kwan, who they can look up to as a strong, successful young man who, with perseverance and hard work, was able to break the mould of what a Chinese man is "supposed" to be: a Chinese man who can jump just as high as anyone else.

And The Tony Award Goes To... Marty Chan

Award winning author (The Mystery Of The Frozen Brains), playwright (Mom, Dad, I'm Living With A White Girl), television writer (The Orange Seed Myth), radio humorist (The Dim Sum Diaries), first playwright in residence at the Citadel Theatre in Edmonton, and Gemini nominee. Marty Chan is the only person I know who carries all these heavyweight titles, and when he agreed to be part of my book, I was thrilled and honoured beyond words. While many people know how wildly successful Marty is, what most don't know is that the inspiration for his award winning touch came from his childhood and family experiences.

Marty's parents were born in mainland China, in the southern region of Guangdong province. His father's family moved to Hong Kong, but his mother's family was still in mainland China in the 1950s, just before the Cultural Revolution. When the Revolution hit in the 1960s, Marty's mother's family left mainland China for Hong Kong. Marty's mother's family had only enough money to get three or four people to Hong Kong, so his grandmother stayed behind, with the promise that she would find a way to reunite with the family later. That promise, however, was never fulfilled. She was caught by the Red Guard and died in one of the 're-education' villages ('re-education' being a euphemism for torture and persecution).

During the Cultural Revolution, the Communist government would force landowners to participate in humiliating and painful acts in an attempt to get them to accept communist ideologies. One method of accomplishing this was through 'criticism circles,' where neighbors and the Red Guard would encircle the "offending" person and yell at them for hours about how worthless they were. Not only did Marty's grandmother go through this, but she was also made to kneel on broken glass.

The 'airplane' or 'jet plane' was another method of torture adopted by Chairman Mao and the Red Guards. In this form of torture, victims were made to kneel and hold their arms out like an airplane—they were required to stay in this position for hours. Shaving half of a victim's head because his or her hairstyle didn't meet the army's approval was also common. Similarly, clothing that didn't meet the army's approval would be ripped from the victim's body. This was a horrible, heartbreaking time in the history of China.

"They say that my grandmother committed suicide," Marty tells me, "because of all the things that happened. But in my subsequent research of the Cultural Revolution, I found that a lot of the people who supposedly committed suicide were actually beaten to death by the

Red Guard. And, of course, the Red Guard were the only witnesses, so, rather than saying, 'We killed them,' they said, 'They committed suicide.'"

On a happier note, when Marty's mother was living in Hong Kong, she found a job in the toy factory that Marty's father owned. Right from their first meeting, Marty's father had a huge crush on Marty's mother. He would send notes to her down the factory line, and she was soon smitten as well. He wanted to take her out, but they had to get past Marty's grandfather first. The couple's solution? Marty's father went all the way up to the seventh floor of the building where Marty's mother lived, knocked on the door, and took off running (he knew Marty's grandfather would answer the door). This was a signal to Marty's mother: if she could get out of the house, past Marty's grandfather, she would throw a piece of paper down from the balcony to the street below, where Marty's dad was waiting. This was her signal that she could meet up with him later. Eventually, of course, the couple came clean with Marty's grandfather and ultimately was married.

I was somewhat floored and a little speechless when Marty told me this story. Yet another of my Chinese stereotypes had been debunked. I had always thought that Chinese marriages during Marty's parents' time were based only on economic and pragmatic reasons. But Marty's story proved me wrong.

Marty tells me that he appreciates this story because, as a child, it gave him an opportunity to see the human side of his parents.

"If you talk to my dad these days, you would have no idea—it would never register that he would be a guy that would actually do something like that. Because he's very... well, he's always asking me if I'm making enough money doing what I'm doing. He's very much like, 'Ok, this is what we need to do. We're done. Okay.'

"But when I hear my mom tell that story, there's a human side to my parents—a side which would make any kid think, 'What? Really? You have an identity beyond me?'"

I tell Marty that he should write a play based on how his parents fell in love.

Marty was born in Edmonton, Alberta. He and his family lived in the Beverly area of Edmonton, three blocks away from two other Chinese families that were friends. The children in the other families were slightly older than Marty, but Marty felt like he belonged.

In the early 1970s, when Marty was six years old, the family moved to Morinville, Alberta, a small town ten miles north of Edmonton, where Marty's father bought Super A Foods—a cross between a grocery store and a butcher shop. The population in Morinville at the time was around 2000, with the Chans being the first Chinese family to put down roots there. The town had a bakery, a machine shop, a grocery store… it was a one of everything (and two gas stations) kind of town. Morinville was small enough that people didn't need to lock their doors or worry where their kids were. Marty tells me that he didn't feel like he needed to let his mom know his whereabouts most of the time.

Many Chinese families with an entrepreneurial spirit gravitate towards small towns to start their new lives. One of the reasons Marty's dad left Edmonton is because there is less competition in small towns—at the time, the Chan's grocery store was the only one in Morinville. His family's ownership of that store has had a significant impact on Marty's life: Marty was an only child at the time, and his younger brother wasn't born until Marty was 15 years old. So during Marty's formative years, his parents worked a lot, and Marty was the only one to help them.

"Because of the responsibility of working in the store, I still feel socially awkward, and most of my time is spent working. The store instilled a certain work ethic in me — I'm used to working 12 to 14 hour days, and I feel guilty if I take a day off. That's because my dad worked every single day. Around that time, they started allowing stores to open on Sundays. So, of course, he opened on Sundays for a few hours. Basically, the idea was that if you're not working, you're not doing anything. Even though I'm a freelancer now, and I can make my own hours, there are days I feel like I should be working and all I'm doing is researching. And I know that researching is working, but because of my dad, I feel like I should be writing all the time.

"My parents' ideal for us was basically raising us to work and find jobs that could support us. Their biggest fear with me being a writer is that when they're gone I won't be able to take care of myself. But I think they're starting to figure out that I can take care of myself regardless of whether I'm a writer or an accountant or anything like that."

Marty also talks about the isolation he felt because of growing up in a small town and the longs hours he worked in the store.

"It's a different experience for me growing up in a small town, simply because I didn't look like other kids at school. In the beginning, I felt quite isolated. I spoke English, but I still didn't feel like I fit in because everybody else was either French or English or Ukrainian or German. There were no other visible minorities the first couple of years that I was there, and I think the kids didn't know what to make of me. I always felt ostracized or put off to the side. I found myself reading a lot when I was in school. This was like a coping mechanism because I felt so nervous."

But Marty wanted desperately to belong.

"One of the things I wanted to do was play on the volleyball team. It was the one thing I was sort of good at. It was the one time the kids would look at me and say that I was pretty good. They thought of me as Marty, as opposed to, 'Oh, he's that strange Chinese kid.' I actually had a great time playing volleyball, but my parents didn't like all the practice times—if I was practicing, I wasn't working at the store. So my parents pressured me to drop volleyball and work in the store. I regret dropping it though, because it was a chance for me to actually be social with the other students. They still had parties, and I was able to go to them, but I never felt connected to anybody because you develop bonds when you're on a team. Because of my responsibility to my parents, and the pressure I felt to work at the store, I found myself socially detached."

The social isolation still affects Marty to this day. "It's carried over. When I talk to people, I tend not to make eye contact. I have the shyness that sort of extended from my upbringing in Morinville. I felt so out of place."

I must note, however, that Marty seemed to have no problem making eye contact with me. And, interestingly enough, while his father's store may have kept him from socializing with other children, it was also the avenue by which he met a lot of the townsfolk. Where he lacked connections with kids his age, he gained connections with the adults who were the customers in his father's store. The customers seemed to find Marty both fascinating and cute.

"When I was in grade three," Marty recalls, "I would stand on a wooden pop crate and actually ring in groceries. Sometimes my dad would stand behind me to make sure I punched in the right numbers. We had the old NCR machines where you needed higher end fingers to work them. I was always afraid of looking stupid in front of the customers. So whenever I didn't know the price of something, and if Dad wasn't standing behind me, I would just make it up. People knew I was undercharging them—I think that's why they were always happy when I was punching in groceries."

I can't help but laugh at Marty's story. "We'll go through Marty's line, thank you," I say, imitating the customers.

"Yeah," Marty laughs with me. "You say it's 13 cents? Oh, okay!"

So it was through those experiences that Marty got to know the folks of Morinville and ultimately felt much more comfortable around adults than he did around kids. Still, Marty kept trying—even without the advantage of belonging to a sports team.

"It took awhile to get the kids to start seeing me as a person," he says. "I spent a lot of time trying to get to know the kids and trying to get them to know me. Initially, there was a really awkward period where the kids just thought I had boogers hanging off of me and would run away from me. But I just kept going at it. I had no other choice—in a small town, it's not like in the big city where you can find a clique that you can hang out with."

It's no wonder Marty had a huge cultural identity crisis when he was growing up.

"During my pre-teen years," Marty tells me, "I kept thinking, 'Why can't I look like the other kids at my school? Why do I have to be Chinese? Why did my parents have to come here?' I questioned why my parents would take me to Morinville and put me through that kind of experience. I didn't understand why. Economically, I could understand they wanted to run a business. But from a social standpoint, I was essentially cut off."

The Caucasian friends that Marty did have when he was growing up were few. And, for the majority of Marty's childhood, there were no other Chinese families in town. When Marty was in grade five, a Chinese family bought a café beside his family's store, but the only child in the new family was a five-year-old girl. And the family didn't stay long—it was only a year or so before Marty's family was once again the only Chinese family in Morinville.

Marty also didn't have much contact with his extended family as he was growing up, although his aunt and uncle did move from Hong Kong to Toronto, and at one point, two of his cousins from Hong Kong came to live with Marty's family and attend school. Marty says he hated them (I can't imagine Marty hating anybody, but that's what he says). But Marty admits that he was young and a tad bit territorial, so there was fierce competition between the "Hong Kong Chinese" and the "Canadian Chinese." Not surprisingly, Marty's cousins didn't like the experience, and shortly after arriving, they returned to Hong Kong. One left earlier than the other, and Marty assumes that he, Marty, probably had something to do with the hasty departure.

Other than that, Marty had only peripheral contact with aunts and uncles, whom he saw once a year when they came into town. But his extended family was, and is, so spread out that it's hard to keep track of them. Obviously, this minimal contact with his extended family played an integral role in separating Marty even further from his Chinese heritage.

Marty's parents were also anxious for Marty to fit into mainstream society. Although Marty's mother spoke Chinese to him, this had little to do with maintaining the Chinese culture: it was simply because she spoke very little English. Thus, Marty spoke Chinese to her, not by choice, but because it was necessary if he wanted to communicate with his mother. Marty's father spoke to him half in English and half in Chinese. But Marty's parents never did send him to Chinese school— nor was there any push for Marty to maintain his Chinese culture. When Marty tells me this, it's with a hint of lingering sadness.

"I'm 41 years old," he says. "And after I left home, I didn't have a lot of exposure to Cantonese, so I've lost a lot. I can sort of understand what people are saying to me, but there's no way I could have a conversation. Now, I can't even really have a conversation with my mom beyond a 'pass the pork' kind of a conversation while sitting at the table. I regret that. In contrast, my brother, who lived at home until he was 26, spoke Chinese to my mom all the time, so they can have meaningful conversations. But I actually have to talk to my mom through my brother sometimes. Sometimes I just throw out an English word to her, hoping she'll understand. She'll kind of nod, and I think, 'Hmmm... I don't know' (if she understood)."

Marty left Morinville when he was 18 and went to the University of Alberta in Edmonton. His parents, perhaps influenced by the Chinese culture, expected him to go into engineering because that's what two of his childhood Chinese friends were doing.

Shortly after starting the program, Marty realized he hated it. On the 9.0 scale that the University of Alberta used at the time, Marty had a grade point average of 1.3. He was kicked out of school, but was ashamed to tell his parents. He simply told them that he didn't like it and had dropped out. Marty worked for a year and then moved back home to Morinville and lived there for a year. But, with his mother harping on him constantly about what he was going to do with his life, he hated every minute of it.

Eventually, Marty realized what his passion was.

"I figured out that I wanted to go back to university and become a writer. In high school, the one thing I loved was writing. And I read so much as a kid that it seemed like a natural fit. Of course, my mom's head spun around 360 degrees because she was like, 'What? Can you make money off of that?' She had a huge, huge fit about it. But I stuck to my guns."

As one can imagine, especially in a Chinese family, Marty's father didn't say much—but his mother was extremely displeased. Even after he finished his Bachelor of Arts degree, Marty's mother still harped at him daily and constantly questioned whether he had made the right decision. This continued even after Marty found work as a writer. Finally, she came around when he started writing and performing the Dim Sum Diaries for CBC (Canadian Broadcasting Corporation) Radio.

"They were three-minute humor pieces," Marty explains, "usually making fun of my mom. As soon as she heard my voice on the radio, she thought, 'Oh, well, if he's on the radio, then he must be making money.' Also, there's that bit of glory that she can hold over her friends. 'Oh, my son's on the radio, what's your son doing?'"

Ironically, neither of Marty's two Chinese childhood friends became engineers either. One became a mechanic, and the other sells mutual funds. Life is funny, isn't it?

Marty's brother, on the other hand, had a totally different relationship with their parents than Marty did. Marty tells me that his brother's relationship with their parents was far less antagonistic. Marty, being the first born, was the 'carrier' of a lot of his parents' hopes, dreams, expectations, and yes, neurosis. In comparison, the expectations placed on Marty's brother were far fewer and less severe. To illustrate this point, Marty tells me a story.

When Marty moved in with his Dutch girlfriend (now wife), Michelle, his mom did more than 'flip.' She claimed that her dreams had been shattered—that her life had fallen apart. Marty and his mother would constantly fight in Chinese at the dinner table with Michelle sitting right there. And even though Michelle doesn't understand Chinese, she could sense the tension via their tones. It even got to the point where Marty's mother would hurl insults at Michelle in Chinese. Eventually, Marty's mother did come around and accept Michelle and her presence in Marty's life—but it took nine years for that to happen.

Yet, when Marty's brother was dating a French girl (now his wife), they would sleep together under Marty's parents' roof—and Marty's mother didn't even blink an eye. In fact, she would often make breakfast for the enamored couple.

It's pretty clear that Marty's brother had it better than Marty did. Marty tells me that the emotional scars from past arguments with his mother still emerge from time to time. And he still worries that one little comment can knock the whole house down.

When Marty tells me this story, it brings to light the fact that both Marty and his brother have married non Chinese women. So this seems like a good time to ask Marty if he believes his upbringing affected his selection of a significant other. Marty tells me it didn't — in fact, prior to meeting Michelle, he says, he dated two Chinese women (at different times, of course). That those relationships didn't last (and that his relationship with his wife did last) had nothing to do with culture, Marty says. Much more important to Marty than culture were connection and having things in common.

When I ask Marty if he would ever consider moving back to Morinville, the differences between Marty's and his brother's experiences are highlighted even further.

"Do I want to go back to live in Morinville? No, not necessarily. For me, I like the town now, but I also love living in the city. I don't like the idea of going to a place where there's limited choices, even though there's more there now than before. But my brother, who's 15 years younger than me, just bought a house in Morinville. He loves being in a small town. So, whatever experiences he had growing up in Morinville were completely different than mine."

There was a time when Marty thought his brother would follow the same path as Marty did, but he didn't. But, Marty points out, his brother, as a child, fitted in much better than he did — after all, there is a 15-year age gap between the brothers. And there are more Chinese people in Morinville, more cultural diversity, and greater acceptance than when Marty was young. For Marty, the racism he experienced in school was direct and personal, and it came from his schoolmates. While Marty's brother did experience racism as well, it was more indirect and subtle, and tended to come from rival schools.

Chink. Chinaman. I think most of the Chinese in Canada have heard these two derogatory words, whether they understand English or not. And Marty was no exception. Although racism was a huge problem initially when he was a child, it virtually disappeared once the other kids got to know him. He tells me that he's not sure if his parents experienced racism. If they did, they've never talked to him about it.

Oddly enough, Marty's experiences with racism became more profound as he grew older. And the racism was often found in the most unexpected places. When he entered university, Marty made it a goal to connect with his Chinese culture more, thinking that this would help him fit in. With this goal in mind, he joined the Chinese Student Association at the University of Alberta, assuming that there would be other Canadian-born Chinese there. But when he went to his first social function, he found that most of the members of the group were from Hong Kong. He also found that, even within the Chinese culture, there are big differences. Within that group of Chinese people, Marty experienced name-calling and ridicule. He was called a 'banana' (white on the inside, yellow on the outside), a 'CBC' (Canadian-born Chinese), and 'white rice.' That experience had a huge impact on Marty. Given his limited contact with other Chinese people when he was growing up, it was a shock for him to find that his first experience with Chinese people en masse was stunted by his first attempt to fit in.

But racism also came from the more usual sources. Just two years ago, right here in Edmonton, Marty merged into a lane while driving and pulled in front of a pick-up truck. The truck whipped around in front of Marty, and, as it was passing Marty's vehicle, the passenger looked out the window at Marty and pulled at his eyes—the classic, derogatory body language for "Chinaman."

But for Marty, the biggest frustration is not outright racism so much as it is the stereotyping that he often encounters in his professional life.

"The one thing that's a source of frustration for me right now is that, when I'm working in theatre and television, a lot of producers will ask me to come up with ideas that are directly related to being Chinese. Those are the kinds of stories that they want me to tell. The producers will talk to me and say, 'We want you to write a story for us, something Chinese.' Or, they come to me and say, 'We've got this great project for you. It's about this Chinese immigrant who comes to Canada.' I'm not sure if that's an overt form of discrimination, but it is stereotyping."

"But you're more than that," I offer.

"Yes. They've created this little box for me," Marty says. "In the beginning of my career in Edmonton, I deliberately chose not to write any plays that had anything to do with being Chinese because I wanted to establish myself as a writer first, not as the Chinese-Canadian writer."

Marty was able to establish this reputation in Edmonton, and it was only when he felt comfortable with his career that he wrote his award winning play, Mom, Dad, I'm Living With a White Girl. This play examines Asian stereotypes and the ordeals of an interracial relationship. It won the Elizabeth Sterling Haynes Award for Best New Work and the Adams Chinese Theatre Award at Harvard University. Marty also hit the big time in the Big Apple when this play was produced by Off Broadway in New York. In short, the play took off, and it soon became the "thing" that Marty is known for. Marty tells me that he's not always comfortable with that fact: he would like to be known as a writer in general, rather than the writer of one particular play.

"I'm enjoying the notoriety that goes with it, but there are times where I kind of wish that people would just say, 'Oh, you're that writer, I've got this great story!'"

"Rather than, 'I've got this great story about the Chinese?'" I ask.

"Right," Marty responds. "Because it kind of limits my creative choices in terms of what people want me to write about. What they will allow me to write about."

Cahoots Theatre Projects, a Toronto company that produces culturally diverse materials, picked up Mom, Dad... and premiered the show in Toronto in 1995. Firehall Arts Centre, a Vancouver company, picked the play up a short time later. Toronto and Vancouver proved to be great cities in which to produce the play, and the tickets were pretty much sold out. Given this, one would think that companies across Canada would be jumping at a chance to produce the play as well, but the response from other cities wasn't nearly as positive.

"What I was getting back from a lot of the artistic directors was, 'Well, you know, this play is only going to work in one of only two cities that have large Asian populations to bring the audiences out,'" Marty explains. "I was really angry at that, and I made it a personal mission to prove everybody wrong. So, I finally convinced the artistic director of Theatre Network, here in Edmonton, to produce the show. It wound up being a huge hit here in the city. And then the theatre companies in middle Canada said, 'Oh, it sold well in Edmonton, then of course we'll pick it up.' So I guess that's another example of discrimination or stereotyping. Even though the characters in the play are Asian, the story is universal. But the art directors of middle Canada saw it only as an Asian story."

As with the other interviewees in the book, I was also curious if Marty has been to China and if so, what are his thoughts on it. Marty has been to China twice. The first time, he says, he was only 11 years old and far too young to appreciate it. All he remembers of that trip is that it was very hot. The second time Marty visited China was in 2000, when a production company was filming a documentary about people who go back to their ancestral lands to look for their cultural roots, and Marty was one of their subjects.

"I went back to try to find the village where my grandmother died," Marty says, "and to talk to some people she might have known. I remember talking to my parents before I left. My parents said, 'No, you'll never find her grave.' They gave me a name and told me what village she grew up in—that's all I had to go on. When we showed up in Toishan, I asked the cab driver, using my limited Cantonese, to find the place. Within 45 minutes, we found where my grandfather's herbal shop had been and somebody who had known him. About an hour later, after finding a translator, we were able to find the village where my grandmother was 're-educated' and her grave. The greatest moment of the trip was when they led me to her grave, and I was able to thank her — if she hadn't sacrificed herself, my mom wouldn't have gotten out, and I wouldn't be here."

Needless to say, this experience has given Marty a bit of a new perspective.

"I think my attitude has changed," Marty tells me. "When I was younger I didn't want to be Chinese or Chinese-Canadian. Now, I know that's who I am, and I'm quite proud of that background. As much as I don't get along with my parents, I'm proud that they chose to come to Canada because if they didn't, I wouldn't have had the experiences that I did. And I would say that I don't have the same identity struggle that I did when I was younger."

Still, while Marty now has friends from many different backgrounds, including Chinese, he maintains that he's not particularly connected to the Chinese culture, except as it pertains to his work.

"I'm not involved with anything specific with the Chinese culture," Marty explains. "I'm trying to find out as much as I can about the head tax and about Chinese opera because it's related to a project (The Forbidden Phoenix) I'm working on. I don't know if that means I want to be involved in the culture — I think it's just the pragmatic side, the work ethic that I was talking about earlier. Anything cultural has to be related to something that makes money. So, if I'm going to learn about this, it's directly related to something I'm working on. Because if I'm only doing it as a hobby, then I'm wasting time."

But there is no denying that Marty's upbringing has had an impact on his occupational choice. And, while his parents' choice of moving to a small town disconnected Marty from the Chinese culture, his occupation as a writer helps him reconnect with that same culture. Marty describes The Forbidden Phoenix as a cross between Chinese opera and North American theatre, and explores the experiences of early Chinese immigrants in Canada and the discrimination they endured in the cold new land. As part of his writing process, Marty conducted intense research in the areas of Chinese opera, myths, martial arts, and the history of the early Chinese immigrants in Canada. And, while this may have seemed like just another part of his work on the surface, it also gave Marty the opportunity to learn a lot about himself.

Overall, Marty feels there's a more general acceptance of the Chinese culture than there was when he was young, and he's proud of Norman Kwong becoming Lieutenant Governor of Alberta. But, he reminds me, there are still people like the guy in the pick-up truck.

Our demographic landscape is changing. Unlike 70 years ago, when the vast majority of the Canadian population was Caucasian, today there are 55,000 to 60,000 Chinese in Edmonton alone. That's not even considering the many other ethnic groups that abound in towns and cities across Canada. But it's still difficult being a visible minority. Racism is driven by fear—fear of the unknown. For this reason, I commended Marty on his children's books: the award winning The Mystery of the Graffiti Ghoul (Thistledown Press, 2006) and The Mystery of the Frozen Brains (Thistledown Press, 2004). Both books carry strong themes of racism, bullying, and overcoming differences. And I strongly believe that if we are to eradicate racism it must start with the children.

Marty tells me that he likes the title of my book. The title is stereotypical, and I purposely chose it for this reason. He's been asked the question before, just like the many times he's been asked if he's related to Jackie Chan, or has been referred to as a bad driver. I'm certainly not as good a playwright as Marty is, but here's my attempt at writing a play nonetheless:

Marty: I'm from Edmonton.

Response: No, no, really, where are you from? Japan? China?

Marty: I'm from Edmonton, Alberta, Canada.

Response: Are the Japanese and Chinese the same? You must be the same. I mean, you all look alike. So where are you from?

Marty: Planet earth, actually. And you?

Cheez Whiz Over Steamed Rice, Please!

When I sit down with 56-year-old Mary Chan, Mary admits to me that she's nervous about our interview. This, she says, is because there are so many missing pieces in her life that she's afraid she won't have much to contribute to my book. As it turns out, she contributes much more than she realizes.

Throughout our interview, Mary touches on a very important concept: regret. Again and again, Mary tells me that she regrets not knowing more about her Chinese history and that she wishes she had asked her parents more questions. There is, she says, this blank space in time that she doesn't know anything about. But, of course, when she was younger, she didn't realize how important it was to ask questions about her culture. And now that she's older, she wishes she did. It is because of this that I dedicate this chapter to my young readers in the hopes that it will inspire them to ask those important questions.

Mary's parents were both born in China, in Toishan county (southeast part of Guangdong province). Mary's father, Jim Pon, originally came to Canada with his parents when he was five years old. But Jim's father eventually returned to China, just as many of the early immigrants planned to do. When it was time, Jim returned to China to wed Mary's mother. Mary's mother, whose name was never Anglicized, didn't set foot in Canada until well after her and Jim had married.

"How old were they when they married?" I ask Mary.

"My father was 21. My mother was 18."

"Was it an arranged marriage?"

"Oh, absolutely," Mary responds. "In those days, nobody would even think of it not being an arranged marriage."

I note there often seems — or at least seemed — to be no such thing as 'getting to know a person,' or as we say today, 'dating' in the traditional Chinese culture. But I have come to learn that arranged marriages are about survival and economic convenience — even to the extent that integrity and dignity go out the door. Because a lot of women in Mary's mother's generation were uneducated and poor, an arranged marriage meant food in their stomachs. It was often a matter of life and death, and there was no room for "getting to know" the person you would wed.

Mary's father stayed in China for a couple of years after the wedding, and then he travelled back and forth between China and Canada. It was during this time that the eldest three of Mary's siblings, two girls and a boy (Allan Pon), were born. Following the birth of the third child, Mary's father was forced to returned to Canada, not only because of World War II, but also, it was the difficulties the Canadian Federal Government were creating for the Chinese in Canada, since The Chinese Immigration Act of 1923. This Act made any Chinese leaving and returning to Canada much more difficult, since the Canadian Government wanted as little Chinese presence in Canada as possible. Between constant separations and the Chinese Exclusion Act, Mary says, her parents really didn't know one another at all.

By the time Mary's mother came to Canada, one of Mary's sisters had died in early childhood, and the other was married with a family of her own and had no desire to leave China (Mary never did meet this sister, who died of bone cancer when she was in her sixties). Thus, only Allan accompanied his mother to Canada. He was 13 years old at the time, and it was not an easy journey.

Mary's father was required to pay the Chinese Head Tax upon his return to Canada. In order to get his family to Canada, Mary's father was forced to purchase what is called a "paper son" for both Allan and his mother. That is, he "bought" his nephew's identity and used it to get his son into the country and "bought" another identity for his wife. This was an expensive procedure, and it was critical that it be done correctly so that immigration officials would have no idea it was happening.

The Chinese Exclusion Act had more than just a financial impact on the Pon family. The huge gap (13 years) prior to the Pon's reuniting in Canada was due, in large part, to the fact that the Canadian Federal Government, for a quarter of a century, refused the Chinese entry into Canada. During this time, only diplomats and merchants were allowed into Canada, and it wasn't until 1947 that the government lifted the ban on Chinese immigrants.

After the Pons finally reunited in Canada, two more children were born. Mary's brother Eddy was born in 1951, and Mary was born in 1952.

I tell Mary that I almost need to draw a family tree because there are so many people involved. But Mary tells me she wouldn't be much help with that.

"I can't tell you these things because my parents didn't talk to me about that. Now everyone is dead, and there's no one left to confirm things. My dad passed away when he was 60, and at the time, I really felt sorry that I didn't know much about our background. My mom didn't pass away until she was 83, but we never talked about stuff like that, which is unfortunate. I have deep regrets over that."

When Mary was a child, she and her family led quite a nomadic life. Mary was born in Donalda, a small Alberta town. She isn't sure how long the family remained there, just as she isn't sure how long they remained in the next place they moved to: Stettler, Alberta. She is also unsure of how her family made a living in Donalda, but she does know that her parents opened a restaurant in Stettler. But that also wouldn't last for long.

"It's like my dad was always planning where our next home would be," Mary says.

When Mary was five years old, the family moved to Fairview, Alberta, and her father once again opened a restaurant in the new location. But this also would turn out to be a short stay: there was already a Chinese restaurant in the town when the Pons arrived, and Mary figures two Chinese restaurants just made for too much competition in one small town. So the Pons moved on.

Next stop was Hines Creek, another small Alberta town, where Mary's father rented a building and opened yet another restaurant. But, when the lease was up, Mary's family moved yet again. This is when the family ended up in Worsley, yet another small Alberta town. Here, Mary's father built his own restaurant rather than renting, and it seemed as if the Pon family might actually establish some roots. The family lived in Worsley from the time Mary was in grade three until the time she was in grade seven. They might have stayed longer, but tragedy struck the family: Mary's father, a severe diabetic, went into a coma and never recovered. After her father's death, Mary's mother, along with Allan, tried to make a go of the restaurant, but it didn't work out. So Mary, along with her brothers and mother, moved to Edmonton.

Mary has never returned to the small towns where her father opened those restaurants. But she does remember quite a bit from those times. She recalls that, while her mother did help out at the restaurant, she generally remained in the back, cooking and cleaning, because she didn't speak English. Thus, it was Mary's father who was present in the front of the restaurant.

So, what were Mary's parent's ideals when it came to raising children? First, Mary points out that her parents were much older than most of Mary's peers' parents.

"My mom didn't come to Canada until she was 44. And Eddy and I were born after that."

Perhaps Mary's parent's ages had something to do with them not wanting their children to be immersed in mainstream society.

"At home," Mary tells me, "we never spoke English. Never, ever, ever. Even if our Chinese was terrible. I know my dad understood English, but he never ever talked to us in English. Ever. And my mother didn't know any English at all. There was a silent understanding that if our parents didn't speak English, neither would we."

On the upside, because she always spoke Toishan with her mother, Mary was able to maintain her Chinese language, at least somewhat, even after her father's death and throughout her young adult life. But maintaining it has become increasingly difficult.

"The bad part is that I don't have much contact anymore with other people who speak Chinese. I talk to the odd person on the bus, but it's usually a mix of something—like half Chinese and half English. And then my accent is lousy because that Canadian accent is always right there. So I'm always thinking, as I speak Chinese, 'Oh my God is she going to laugh at me?'

"Sometimes it comes out pretty good, and then people will say, 'Oh, were you born in China?' And when I explain that I was born here (in Canada), they say, 'Oh—well how come your Chinese is so good?'"

Mary laughs at this point. "It's not good, and I know it's not good, but I am trying to practice more."

I tell Mary that I think it's rare and wonderful that she's still able to speak the language, in spite of being born in Canada.

That is the upside of Mary being forced to speak only Chinese in her family home. On the downside, she often found it difficult to communicate with her parents, since English words and concepts don't always translate well into Chinese.

"I remember," Mary says, "wanting Cheez Whiz so bad. But I didn't know how to tell them that in Chinese. So I got Velveeta Cheese instead. I was sick and tired of Velveeta Cheese. I wanted Cheez Whiz because it's nice and smooth, and you can spread it around easily on toast. But I couldn't tell them that — I didn't know how. So we just kept going with whatever they knew. There was no selection at all. If you were sick and tired of eating rice everyday, too bad. You couldn't say, 'We're sick and tired of this.' And my mom didn't read — she was completely illiterate — so she couldn't use recipes. We more or less ate whatever she could think of, and there was no way we could refuse."

Mary's father also drilled into Mary and Eddy's heads the idea that hamburgers were made from horsemeat. So the children weren't allowed hamburger (although he had no problem serving it to customers in the restaurant). While Mary and her brothers were allowed an occasional (very occasional, Mary stresses), chocolate bar, chips were strictly off limits.

"What did you eat?" I ask Mary.

"We always had Chinese food, and we always had rice. Always rice, and it was always steamed rice, no fried rice."

Mary notes that, since her family owned a restaurant, you would think that they (the children) would have access to all the junk food they wanted — or at least be given a ration. But this wasn't the case for Mary and her brothers.

I offer Mary two theories about this: 1) perhaps her parents knew the lack of nutritional value in junk food; or 2) perhaps her parents associated junk food with "white mainstream society," and they didn't want their children to become "white."

Mary says she doesn't know which, if either, of these two possibilities was the case. Either way, she and her brothers did, from time to time, "sneak" junk food by purchasing it secretly with their spending money.

I ask Mary if there were other ways in which her family owning a restaurant impacted her.

"I'm not sure," Mary says. "We (the children) never really helped out at the restaurant. The only thing I ever really did for them was order magazines — that's because I was the only one who could read English. I mean, besides Eddy, but he really didn't care about the magazines. Actually, we spent a lot of our time fooling around and playing.

"We lived right behind the restaurant. It was really funny. My mom and dad saw each other from morning until night 365 days of the year. Nowadays, we would say, 'God, we need a break from one another!' and my parents probably thought that too, but they didn't have much choice. And I don't think they really knew each other. My mom got married at 18. How could she know my dad? My dad didn't even stay there (in China), not for even two years in a stretch. Maybe a little over a year and a half, then he came back to Canada, then he went back to China, and they had my brother (Allan), and then he came back here because of the war. My mom didn't know my dad."

I ask Mary if she felt like she fit in at school when she was a child, and she tells me that she didn't. She and Eddy, were the only Chinese kids at school, and, in all of the small towns that her family lived in, they were the only Chinese people in town.

"There were a lot of (First Nations)," Mary tells me, "but most of the people there were of Ukrainian background. But the (First Nations) really stood out too. I think they were just as awkward as we were."

Mary tells me that her family definitely experienced racism when she was growing up.

"I really felt more for my parents than for myself," she says. "I didn't really have much to do with the restaurant, but I know that my parents had a lot of problems with customers. They would mimic us and make fun of our language."

Mary's parents, like so many other immigrants, were simply trying to carve out a new life in a new land. And they had no choice but to keep working hard (the welfare system is a foreign concept in China and in the Chinese culture) and just "put up with" the abuse.

For Mary herself, racism came mostly in the form of name-calling when she was a little girl.

"Nothing was thrown at me or anything. Just a lot of name-calling. When I look back at it, I think it was just immaturity. These were close-minded people who didn't even think about whether they were hurting someone's feelings. They just thought it was okay as long as it wasn't happening to them. It was part of being in the 'in' crowd. And I'm sure there may be some of them who make fun of us behind our backs. But they don't do it to me in front of my face."

"I suppose," I say, "that in a small town, you were always the minority. And, because you had no one to protect you, it was easy for them to gang up on you. But now, not only are there more Chinese people, there are also laws against discrimination and harassment. So did you find that it changed when you moved to the city?"

"When I first started working as a cashier," she says, "I would get remarks from customers. But many of them hadn't seen a Chinese cashier before. But now they're used to me: there's such a high turnover where I work, but I'm still there. And so they accept me."

In general, Mary is pretty much resigned to the existence of racism.

"It's never, ever going to go away," she says. "That's the way it is. It may not be as direct as when I was a child, but you can still feel it. And it will be that way forever. Even down the road, even three or four generations from now, it's still going to be there. As long as there are different nationalities, there will be racism."

Still, Mary does believe that there is a higher level of tolerance in the city than there was in the small towns she grew up in. This, she believes, is because people in cities are more accustomed to seeing a mosaic of cultures around them. Also, she points out, people are more educated now.

Speaking of education, I ask Mary what her parents' views were on that particular subject. She tells me that they didn't emphasize education at all—either for her or for her brother Eddy. (I thought perhaps Mary's parents would have considered education more important for Eddy given that sons are usually more valued than daughters in Chinese families.)

Mary points out that it may have been that her parents didn't encourage education simply because they didn't really know what it entailed, never having experienced it themselves.

"It's not because they didn't care about us," Mary says. "My father couldn't really read English, but he knew the numbers, and he didn't have any training or education at all. He came here when was five years old, and he didn't go to school. He worked and worked and worked, until he died."

As for Mary's mother, she also had no formal education. This, of course, was right in line with the Chinese philosophy (as opposed to the individualistic philosophy of the West) that a woman's role is that of wife and mother. And once a woman is married, she doesn't need an education—her husband will take care of her (as opposed to the modern day values of higher education and leverage for women).

It is partially because of this family philosophy that Mary (and Eddy as well) never went beyond grade twelve. I ask Mary if she thinks her educational status and her occupation as a cashier at a major grocery chain steer her away from, or bring her closer, to her cultural roots.

"Definitely away," Mary says. "Not many Chinese people work as cashiers at (major) grocery stores, unless their families own the business. Also, the store I work in is outside of Chinatown, so I don't see a lot of Chinese customers."

When Mary tells me that she has only her high school diploma, she is slightly, though visibly, embarrassed. I quickly assure her that it's not a big deal — and that I've met people with little education who are much wiser and have far better people skills than many people who have degrees coming out of their ears. There is, I say, something to be said for not basing your entire identity on your educational status.

I do feel compelled, however, to point out that there are Chinese people who would disagree with me. There are many for whom the extent of one's education and how much one has in his or her bank account is of top priority. And it's not that I'm trivializing the importance of money: it's just that I tend to agree with Mary when she says that the Chinese culture puts too much emphasis on it. As a case in point, I share with Mary how, at my grandmother's funeral, a cousin of mine approached me and started a conversation. But, rather then seizing the opportunity to reminisce about our grandmother, he asked me how much money I made.

As Mary points out, however, there may be a good reason that this philosophy has become engrained in the Chinese culture.

"When I was growing up," she says, "all of the Chinese people had to make sure they had enough money to send some back home to relatives in China. I always thought we were really poor. When our parents bought us clothes, it didn't really matter what size we were; they always made us buy clothing that was way too big so that we could grow into it. And that was only once a year, and we just got the basics. The clothing just had to cover us and that's it; as long as our bums weren't showing, that was good enough. So, yeah, I thought we were poor. But actually they were sending money back home — and that's the way it had to be. You have to look after your own people."

And the idea that young people who are able to work have a duty to take care of their elders is deeply embedded in Chinese culture. The money that Mary's parents sent to China definitely went to Mary's grandparents, and extended family received a bit as well. Mary isn't sure how much money her family sent, but she says it must have been fairly substantial because her grandfather was able to save enough money to buy six buildings, which he still owns.

So, unless all of one's relatives and family members have moved out of China, there was (and still is) a strong expectation that the family in the new country will send money back to the family in the ancestral land. I mentioned to Mary that this often puts a tremendous amount of pressure on the oldest son of a family or the head of a household and may be one of the contributing factors to a lot of the mental illness that is overlooked in Chinese communities. After all, running a business, raising a family, making mortgage payments, and supporting another family back in China requires a lot of juggling.

So, while Mary's family wasn't poor, they didn't dare treat themselves to a T-bone steak for fear of becoming that way. And while the Pon family never went hungry, they also never had the opportunity to splurge. It breaks my heart knowing that so many immigrants work so hard, and yet, money is always tight. And the discrimination against the "poor" in the Chinese community doesn't help. It's bad enough that these people have to work tirelessly to support so many people, but they are also expected to become rich themselves. And no matter which way they turn, there's stress that they can't get away from.

"It's amazing and sad how much your family had to sacrifice," I say to Mary.

"Absolutely," she responds. "I think that's why my dad died so early — he never looked after himself. He was the oldest. He had to make sure the money got sent back. We weren't starving, but we didn't eat as well as we should have, even though we owned a restaurant. And we wore clothes that didn't fit us. We may not have been poor, but it sure felt like it."

Although the presence of extended family back in China certainly had a direct impact on Mary's life, there was no extended family directly involved in her day-to-day life. Of all of Mary's parents' siblings, only one aunt and one uncle ever came to Canada. (Mary isn't certain when, exactly, that was.) Mary's uncle died working on the Canadian railroad. (Mary inserts here that she thinks that all of those who worked on that railroad should have free passes for life because, without them, the railroad would never have been built.) And Mary's aunt (her mother's sister) elected to go to Saskatchewan rather than Alberta. Because both Mary's aunt and Mary's mother were illiterate, and a telephone was a luxury neither could afford, there was no interaction between the two. In fact, the only way a message made it from one to the other was if someone they both knew happened to be in a position to deliver it. This was the case when, after a 16-year separation, someone informed Mary that her sister had moved to Vancouver, and the two were finally able to reconnect.

That said, there were plenty of people in Edmonton with the "Pon" surname. And, while they weren't necessarily related to one another (and Mary wasn't related to any of them, other than her brothers and mother), many of them lived within Edmonton's small Chinatown, and they did socialize with one another.

From here we turn to the subject of marriage. I wonder what Mary's parents' attitudes were toward this topic, given that they were such traditionalists.

"I was brought up to believe you have no choice," Mary tells me. "You get married, period. You certainly don't ever say 'I'm not getting married.'"

"That's what was drilled into your head?" I ask.

"Yes. I had to get married. Absolutely."

"How old were you when they started telling you that?"

"It's not that they told me," Mary explains. "You just understand it. You get married, Nancy—every human being, regardless of whether they're insane or not normal, or missing limbs, or whatever... you still get married."

To emphasize her point, Mary tells me that even her second eldest sister—the one who died young and whom Mary never met—was married.

"When she [would have been 16], they (Mary's parents) found a matchmaker. And the matchmaker found another family whose son had died. Then the two, my [deceased] sister and the other family's deceased son, were married. Everyone gets married—at least spiritually."

"Wow," I respond, in a bit of a state of shock, "that's mind-blowing."

And I have to admit to Mary that it all sounds a bit creepy to me. She, however, is resigned to the realities of many Chinese traditions. "You don't stay single—dead or alive, sane or insane, able bodied or handicapped—you just don't stay single. That's the way it is."

Not surprisingly, no one in Mary's family is married to a non-Chinese person. No "ifs, ands, or buts!" as Mary puts it.

"Everyone in the family had to marry Chinese," she says. "Marrying outside of that was just something we couldn't do."

"And was that expectation also unspoken?" I ask.

"Yes," she says. "I'm not sure how we knew, but we knew. And it wasn't just with marriage. At school, we could talk to the Caucasians, but we couldn't really 'mingle' with them."

"You couldn't have Caucasian friends?" I ask.

"Not to bring home," she says.

"So, since you and Eddy were the only Chinese kids in town, does that mean you never, ever brought friends home?"

"No. Never."

So, whether it be marriage or social connections, the idea that it was necessary to remain within the walls of one's own cultural group had roots that ran deep in Mary's family.

Mary is no longer married. Although her marriage was not arranged (she met her ex-husband at a drugstore where she was working at the time), that doesn't mean, Mary points out, that pressure didn't play a part in her decision to marry him. It was a given, she says, that she HAD to marry and that the man she married HAD to be Chinese, so her choices were somewhat limited.

I don't even bother to ask the question of whether Mary believes her experiences as a Chinese person growing up in Canada affected her choice of a mate. Clearly, the answer is "Yes!"

Currently, Mary isn't involved in any activities that have anything to do with her Chinese heritage. Mary has two daughters: one is 30 and the other 25. When her girls were young, Mary tells me, she put the eldest into Chinese school. But the timing was wrong. By this time, Mary was raising the girls on her own, and they had to be put in an English-speaking daycare. And, while Mary did try to enroll her youngest daughter in Mandarin classes when she was in grade seven, it was, by then, too late. Mary's daughter was already too far behind the other children in the class, many of who had been in Chinese school since kindergarten.

As the girls were growing up, Mary spoke to them in English, which she still does today. When the girls were little, they were exposed to a bit of the Chinese language because their grandmother, of course, spoke to them in Chinese.

I ask Mary if she encourages her children, now, to be active in the Chinese lifestyle.

"No," Mary tells me, "My kids don't even associate with the Chinese. None of their boyfriends are Chinese. I thought the younger one would be more interested in a Chinese person, but, no."

So it would seem that, in spite of the traditional upbringing Mary received, neither she nor her children identify in any substantial way with the Chinese culture. This makes me wonder about her brother Eddy (Mary is not close to Allan) and his reaction to what was, essentially, the same upbringing. Interestingly, Eddy seems to have moved in the opposite direction.

"It's a bit different for me," Mary says, "because I've been divorced for 26 years. But Eddy is married to a woman who is actually from China. He's 110% pure Chinese. His wife speaks both Cantonese and Toishan, so she's a huge help to Eddy in maintaining the language. And their kids also speak fluent Chinese, and they are surrounded by extended family, which helps reinforce the language. Also, because Eddy was the son and I was the daughter, he was the one who stayed with my mother — even after he was married, he stayed with her, so my mother's Chinese mentality sort of transferred to him. He has hardly any Canadian in him at all — pure Chinese!"

At this point, Mary stops and laughs. "When Eddy's family fights, they rattle off just as if they were in China. It makes me think I would hate to be married to someone that fluent in Chinese — I would lose every single argument!"

But this is not to say that Mary has put away everything Chinese. She has, in fact, been to China three times. And, she tells me, she learns more each time she's there.

"I often go on tours," she says, "but the problem with that is that they don't expose you to anything they don't want you to see. So they dictate what you learn. You just don't see the 'real' China or the China you would see if you were there with relatives."

The first time Mary went to China, which included a visit to Hong Kong, she was 18 years old. At the time, Hong Kong wasn't yet a part of China (this was prior to 1997, which is when England handed Hong Kong back to China). On this visit, Mary travelled with a classmate.

"I thought the trip was one of the biggest wastes of time," Mary tells me.

I'm sure the surprise shows on my face. "Why?" I ask.

"Well," Mary explains, "we spent most of our time with my classmate's relatives. And you hope that when you see the relatives they'll take you sightseeing or give you a 'real' tour of the place. But they didn't do that—I actually think they were too cheap. And then we saw some of my relatives, but, again, we didn't go anywhere special. And I didn't want to just sit around and talk—what was I going to talk to them about?"

The second time Mary went to China was when she was in her midforties. Again, she went to mainland China and concentrated on seeing the touristy areas. And then Mary took a third trip just a few years ago, which included a visit to Tibet.

As stated earlier in the book, in Raymond Breton's significant 1964 article on "institutional completeness", he argues that institutional completeness keeps the immigrants' social relations within ethnic boundaries, thus heightening their ethnic identity. As for the people Mary surrounds herself with at home, her physician and dentist are both Chinese—though both are established outside of Chinatown, and her physician actually grew up in Poland. "A Chinese doctor who speaks English with a Polish accent," Mary says, laughing. And, she says, her accountant is Dutch—so she doesn't think there's a real conscious effort on her part to choose professionals of any particular ethnicity.

It's pretty clear that Mary experienced a cultural identity crisis when she was growing up. And, in many ways, she still feels that push and pull between cultures. When she was young, she didn't want to know as much about the culture as she did. Now that she's older, she wishes she knew more. Still, she says she feels more Chinese-Canadian now.

"Absolutely, I experienced a crisis," Mary says. "But don't forget, in those days it was rare to see a Chinese person. People weren't as open minded as they are now. Now, people are more educated and tolerant of cultural diversity. And the Chinese have made a name for themselves: 80-85 percent of our products are made in China.

That's how much we have progressed. When I was young, I stuck out like a sore thumb. But now I feel like I stick out because I'm part of a visible majority instead of a visible minority. And I still have some confusion, but I think I feel more mature and sure about my cultural identity now."

Mary tells me that she likes the title of my book, and she feels that there is still a lot of ignorance when it comes to her Chinese heritage.

"People always asks me," Mary says, "how long I've been here (in Canada). And I tell them I was born here, but they still keep asking, as if they didn't hear my answer the first time. And then there are the Chinese people from China who, when they find out I was born here, ask immediately if I can speak Chinese, or if I eat hamburgers every day. So it definitely comes from both sides."

As we wrap up the interview, Mary reminds me again of how nervous she was about it. And she still isn't sure that she had anything worthwhile to say. But I believe she has had a remarkable life thus far, and I tell her that I have a gut instinct that I will be using her story.

The first few times I met Mary, I had no idea she had been born in a small Alberta town. And she is extremely modest, so even once we started talking, and she started to reveal bits of her background, she kept downplaying the significance of the events in her life. But I had a hunch this feisty woman with an infectious laugh carried with her a story that was both fascinating and intriguing. And now I'm sure of it.

The Sky's The Limit

Mental note: Don't forget to bring up Mr. K (a friend of mine) attending a 1956 football game where Norman played against the Saskatchewan Roughriders at Edmonton's Clarke Stadium…

… yeah, no problem.

Don't forget to curtsy, as he is the Queen of England's representative (so I was reminded, though by whom I don't remember) …

… okay, no problem.

The Sky's The Limit

I race up the huge, elongated steps of the Alberta Legislature on my way to meet a very important man for an interview I thought would never happen. In my rush and my dither, I almost twist my ankle. A group of tourists heading toward me gasps in unison, anticipating the spectacular fall I'm about to take. At the last minute, I manage to recapture my balance so, I don't fall on my face. But I also forget to mention the 1956 football game during the subsequent interview (sorry Mr. K), and I forget all about curtsying. I am pretty much a wreck.

So who is this man who has my feathers so ruffled, even before the interview begins?

His name is Norman L. Kwong. And most people who haven't been living under a rock will recognize him not only for being one of the greatest Edmonton Eskimo football players of all time, but also for becoming the first Chinese Lieutenant Governor of Alberta, in 2005. His full title is "His Honour, the Lieutenant Governor, the Honourable Norman L. Kwong, CM, AOE." As legendary as his football career is, as great an accomplishment as it was to be named to the Order of Canada in 1998, and as truly admirable it is that he was the 16th Queen's representative for the Province of Alberta from 2005 to 2010, this chapter focuses more on his younger years and his experiences with the Chinese culture.

Also with us during our interview is Norman's wife, Mary Kwong (nee Lee), who is even more stunning, more breathtaking, than she is in pictures I've seen of her in her younger years. Unlike many of the experiences I have with other Chinese women, where the conversation is loud, almost like a competition, I find Mary to be soft spoken and extremely articulate. She puts me immediately at ease.

Norman begins by telling me about his father. When Charles Kwong first came to Canada from China to work on the railroad in the early 1890s, he and most other Chinese men of the time wore their hair in a long braid.

"I've seen pictures of Chinese men with their hair in a braid in history books," I say.

"Yes," Norman responds. "They were teased about it mercilessly. I even remember reading incidents where the Caucasian workers would physically cut the Chinese worker's braided hair off." But Norman isn't sure if this happened to his father. If it did, his father never mentioned it.

Charles and Lily Kwong, Norman's parents, came to Canada separately in the 1920s. Both were from the Toishan/Canton area in the southern part of China. Charles worked on the Canadian railroad from Vancouver to Calgary, and Lily lived in Victoria, British Columbia, with her family. Through an arranged marriage, they met and married in Victoria.

Mary sees the horror on my face when I hear the phrase 'arranged marriage', and she offers a story of her own.

"My mom and dad," Mary tells me, "also didn't know each other — although they knew of each other — until the day of their wedding. And now they've been married for 60 years."

Charles and Lily settled in Calgary, Alberta, and Norman was born there in 1929. There were approximately 1,200 Chinese people and visible minorities in Calgary during the 1930s and 1940s, which would have been Norman's formative years. This was a reflection of the racist Canadian laws that prohibited Chinese people from entering Canada starting in 1923 and finally lifted in 1947. Naturally, cultural diversity was a foreign concept to many.

Mary and Norman both recall that during the Second World War, because the Chinese and Japanese were the most distinctive Asian populations in Canada, members of those two populations were required to wear pins or badges so they could be readily identified. Mary has kept her pin to this day.

Norman's parents owned a grocery store when Norman was a youngster. He describes what this was like for him.

"We'd gone through the Great Depression of course and that meant that things weren't as plentiful, or the standard of living wasn't as high, as now. But other than that, it was a normal way of growing up."

Norman remembers his father being a very generous man. When customers were unable to pay for something at the store, Norman's father would tell them it was okay—they could pay next time. And most of them did.

Coincidentally, Mary's father also owned a grocery store. Although Mary's father's store was in Vancouver's Chinatown and carried mainly herbs as opposed to milk and vegetables, generosity was a common thread between the two storeowners. During the Second World War, cash and coupons were used to pay for rationed items such as butter and sugar, and Mary clearly remembers her family giving these valuable coupons to other families in need.

When Mary mentions that her father had many, many Caucasian clients in Vancouver and was friends with many of them, Norman can't help but tease her a bit. "Yeah," he says, "that's because they all owed him money."

In spite of the hardships of the Depression, however, having parents who owned a grocery story definitely had it perks. Norman tells me he often felt like royalty because he had access to food and candy that most kids could only dream of. When Norman tells me this, I can't help but ask if his friends felt any resentment toward him because of this.

"I don't think so," Norman says. "My friends knew we had the store, and most of their parents worked for the CPR (Canadian Pacific Railroad). Nobody had a lot of money in the 20s, 30s, or 40s, but I don't think there was any resentment. And as soon as I went into high school,

I encountered the mainstream population— where there were some people who were very wealthy and others who weren't."

Since Norman rarely worked in the store, this left time for him to develop other interests.

"My parents didn't really pressure us to work there (in the store)," Norman says. "I was lucky because I was the fifth child. The older ones, of course, had to work, but I rarely did, so I had time to play. That's how I got involved in sports, I think."

When Norman was growing up, his family was one of two Chinese families in the Calgary neighborhood they lived in. Although Norman's father worked for the father of the other family, Norman didn't spend a lot of time with this other family. The girls were close to Norman's age, but he didn't like playing with girls at that age, and the one boy in the family was 20 years older than Norman. This, combined with Norman's interest in sports, resulted in him hanging out more with the Caucasian kids in the neighborhood.

Norman also had very little extended family in Calgary when he was growing up. "Although we had family friends who were Chinese in Crossfield and in Olds, they weren't blood relatives. Because they were Chinese, and they had children the same age as us, we became friends, but I didn't see them all that often—maybe once a month, a little more during the summer."

This minimal interaction with other Chinese families didn't help Norman maintain his Chinese culture.

I ask Norman what his parents' ideals were when it came to raising Norman and his siblings. Like most traditional Chinese families, Norman tells me, the elder Kwongs wanted the children to focus on eduction. Mary once again points to the similarities between her family and Norman's when she adds, "In those days, they didn't talk about health. They didn't talk about running a block a day."

"How did your parents react when you said, 'Mom, Dad, I love football. I'm going to play for the CFL (Canadian Football League)?'" I ask Norman.

"It didn't really come about that way," he says. "When I played sports, it was a natural progression of playing in junior and then senior high school. I never consulted with my parents on any of those moves. The opportunities just came along, and I took them. I think because I was the fifth child, they didn't really pressure me one way or another."

"What about the rest of your siblings?" I ask.

"I think there was more pressure on the oldest sister, being the first born, and the two oldest brothers," he says.

I ask Norman if he or his parents experienced racism when he was growing up, and he tells me that he has no recollection of his parents sharing any racism they may have encountered. And, Norman says, the family store was never targeted. The Kwong family was fully accepted into the neighborhood. This, Norman suggests, could be because most of the people in their neighbourhood were not wealthy, and they showed respect to the Kwongs because Norman's father was a successful man. As for Norman himself, he does remember one particular incident—an incident Norman previously recounted in the March 26, 2007 edition of the Herald Tribune.

"It was a time," Norman says, "when I don't think I was even in school yet. I was under six years old. We went to Rotary Park, as it was called. There was a wading pool there, and I asked my sister, 'Can we go in the wading pool?' 'No,' she said. 'Why?' I asked. 'Because we're Chinese,' she said.

"This stuck with me. I forget now if there was a sign there or not. There might have been," Norman says.

Mary then adds her own recollection of a story Norman once told her. "Norman's sister wanted a job at Eaton's or The Bay, but she couldn't get one because she was Chinese."

Norman nods in agreement. "They outright told her that," he says.

As for racism that was directed toward Norman in particular, Norman says that he's lucky in that he never really experienced a whole lot of it — and actually didn't think about it all that much.

"I never really thought about being different from my classmates or my friends," he says. "I played softball — it was called fastball in those days — and we sometimes went to the smaller communities to play, and I would sometimes get called different names and things like that. I used to resent it of course, but I didn't do too much about it. My teammates always stuck up for me whenever something like that happened."

"What about when you were older — out on the road?" I ask.

"Right at the very start," Norman tells me, "we (the team) were checking into a hotel, and one of the people checking us in made it clear that I wasn't welcome in their hotel. Of course, he had nothing to do with it, really — he was just a clerk doing his job. Other than that one incident, though, I was largely accepted wherever I went because I was part of the sporting team."

Norman does admit that he encountered a bit of name calling from competing teams, but, for the most part, it was all just part of the game. For instance, Norman remembers being directly targeted only once in the 10-12 years he played. But that, he says, was because he knocked an opponent down during the game. So, he maintains, it was not about being Chinese; it was about the game. Mary suggests that a large part of the reason Norman didn't experience a lot of outright racism was that he was so well respected for his legendary play on the football field.

Norman adds that black players experienced the same situations he did. "But," he says, "the only time I really noticed was when we were checking into hotels. And it was always right at the very start of their careers that something like that would happen. Once they were accepted as part of the team, the racism stopped." These moments were inevitable, Norman suggests, and they usually waned as the players become more successful and respected.

This is not to say, however, that racism isn't still a problem. Mary and Norman tell me that, not long ago, their youngest son encountered name calling while playing ball in Hobbema, a small Alberta town.

In general, however, Mary and Norman say that racism is not really an issue for their four boys, who seem to get along well with everybody. In fact, when one of the boys was in China, a Chinese interpreter asked him if he got along with the Caucasian people in Canada. Norman and Mary's son's response was simple, and telling. "Of course!" he said.

So much for racism. But what about culture? After all, not many people—never mind Chinese people—ever become football stars. So I'm compelled to ask if Norman, as a visible minority in the CFL, ever felt a tug-of-war between the Canadian and the Chinese cultures.

"No," he says. "Not at all. Mostly because of the way I was raised. I was largely without a Chinese culture."

"But I think," Mary adds, "that he was always proud to be a Chinese football player. He might not have come right out with it, or verbalized it, but I know he's proud."

Norman nods thoughtfully, and I can't help but agree with Mary. It would seem that, although Norman just focused on and played the game he loved, he was—and is—very proud to be Chinese. He just doesn't need the bells and whistles and banners to prove it. It's in his heart.

Obviously, Norman spent much more time with Caucasians than he did with other Chinese people. But what about romance? I ask Norman if his experience growing up as a Chinese person in Canada had any influence on his decision making when it came to the cultural background of his wife.

In response to this question, Norman tells me that there was an unspoken and silent expectation from his parents that he would marry Chinese.

Mary tells me that her mother had the same expectations. "I couldn't go out with a Caucasian," she says. "I could have Caucasian friends, but not boyfriends. Then again, there were more Chinese in Vancouver than there are here, so there was always some Chinese function we could go to where I could meet people.

"That's just the way it was then," Mary continues, "I had to marry a Chinese guy. But, anyway, I think I did okay."

We all stop to laugh at Mary's statement. Indeed, not only did Mary do "okay," it would seem that Norman and Mary's relationship was somewhat predestined. In fact, in 1956, when Mary and Norman were dating, Norman got word that he was to fly to Calgary for a game, and that his seat was booked on Flight 810. But, because he had a date with Mary, Norman cancelled his flight. As fate would have it, Flight 810 never made it to Calgary: it crashed into Mount Slesse in British Columbia, killing all 62 people on board. So it would seem that Mary and Norman's stars were aligned—at least that day.

Back to the topic at hand, however, Norman tells me that his youngest brother, Richard, married a non-Chinese person in spite of any unspoken "rules" about such things. But Richard was among a minority.

"In those days," Mary says, "very few Chinese people did that. My mother used to say to me 'I'd rather you marry a Japanese (than a Caucasian)' because at least they're of Asian heritage. And the fact is that when Richard got married, his mom and dad didn't approve of it. They just got married anyway."

"Was there a big reaction from any of your other relatives?" I ask Norman.

"No," he says, "there wasn't any outright rebellion. They just sort of accepted it."

And as interracial marriage becomes more and more common, Mary and Norman agree that acceptance is growing within the Chinese community. Mary's father's attitude is a prime example of this.

"Even though I wasn't allowed to date non Chinese," Mary says, "when I told my dad that my son was dating a Caucasian, he just said, 'Oh, that's nice.' Of course, I didn't know if he really, really meant it, so I said to him, 'You know what, Dad? If he was going out with a girl who I didn't like and you didn't like, that would be much worse!'" Well said, Mary!

In fact, two of Norman and Mary's four sons have married Caucasians.

"We're quite international," Mary says. "We have four daughters-in-law: one is Dutch, one is Czechoslovakian, one is Taiwanese, and one is Chinese."

From the subject of marriage and culture, we turn to the subject of language. Norman tells me that he spoke very little Chinese at home as he was growing up. Because Norman's parents both worked at the store and interacted with the English-speaking population, there was little need for Norman to learn Chinese. I ask him if he ever spoke Chinese with any of the other Chinese families he came into contact with.

"I don't remember speaking Chinese to them," he answers. "Must have been English. I didn't know Chinese."

Mary, on the other hand, had more opportunity to practice the language. Although her father did speak English, her mother, because she was always at home raising the children and had very few opportunities to interact with mainstream society, didn't speak English at all.

I ask Norman how he feels about not being able to speak the language.

"I don't miss being able to speak it," he says.

Mary, however, has a bit of a different perspective on this topic.

"Just before we got married," she tells me, "we were sitting in the living room, and I got up to go get something in another room. He (Norman) said to me, 'Don't you leave me!' And I said, 'Why?' He said, 'Your mother is going to talk to me.' But I left anyway. And he did a good job. He can do it when he has to."

I ask Norman if he thinks that if I, or someone else, were to speak Chinese to him, he could understand it. He tells me, quite adamantly, that he doesn't think so. But, again, Mary disagrees.

"It's not that you don't know anything," she says to him. "You do. Like my dad, he speaks English and Chinese. He's gone now, but when we used to go to Vancouver when he was alive, he (Norman) would speak Chinese to my dad. And that wasn't that long ago. I think when he is forced to speak it, he can. He just needs a little push."

I ask whether any of Norman and Mary's four sons attended Chinese school, and they tell me that two of them did, but they didn't like it. When I ask why, they tell me that it didn't work out because the teacher spoke only Chinese, and the boys spoke only English. "The boys cried and didn't want to go back," Mary tells me.

The other two boys didn't attend Chinese school at all. Mary is a bit regretful about this fact. "I should have continued," she says, "because now the two boys who did attend would like to learn how to speak it. And they have teachers who speak English now. Back then, though, it was harder to find teachers who spoke both languages: there was a smaller Chinese population and less demand."

Mary and Norman, of course, both speak English at home. But, Mary says, when it comes to food, the family still uses the Chinese names for traditional dishes—chow fan for stir-fried rice noodle and lap cheong for seasoned sausage, for instance.

The Kwongs also aren't involved in a lot of Chinese celebrations or functions. "Maybe two percent of the things we do are Chinese related," Norman tells me.

The couple does, however, belong to a Chinese association in Calgary. This particular association, however, is not a cultural club or gathering, and the language of choice is English. While the association does celebrate the Chinese New Year, there is no ancestral worship, exchange of Chinese recipes, or passing down of Chinese folklore. Instead, the association concentrates on activities such as fundraising for university scholarships.

Although the couple has visited Hong Kong, they have never been to mainland China. And, while Mary says that she would go if the opportunity ever presented it, it would seem that Norman has had his fill of travelling.

"I just don't care to travel anywhere," he tells me.

When I ask His Honour if he thinks that cultural acceptance has improved in Alberta, he tells me that he believes it has, and that cultural diversity is an important part of the Alberta landscape.

"I don't think cultural diversity is the 'strange' thing it used to be. And there's still a ways to go in eradicating racism, but I don't think it's as big of a problem as it used to be. When I go to school now, I look out into the audience and maybe 25 percent of the people are Caucasian, whereas it used to be that there were maybe two percent who weren't. So it has to get better, because the Caucasians are outnumbered now. The stats have changed dramatically, and we simply can't afford racism."

When I first met Norman at the 2005 Installation Dinner, where he was sworn in as the Lieutenant Governor of Alberta, there was a throng of celebrities present, including former Edmonton Mayor and

Edmonton Eskimo Bill Smith, sports announcer Brian Hall, philanthropist Sandy MacTaggart, and Norman's former teammate Jackie Parker. But as star struck as I was at the event, it was Norman's speech about fighting racism in Alberta and building a better future for our children that has stayed with me to this day. At the time, I didn't know much about football (and I still don't), and I didn't know much about this man who made history over and over again. But what I do know for sure is that this man has set the sky as the limit. After meeting and getting to know Norman Kwong, I am prouder of being Chinese, and he had inspired me to reach for the sky in whatever I am doing.

Both Mary and Norman are soft-spoken, warm, welcoming people with a delightful sense of humour. It didn't take long for me to feel comfortable with them—like old friends. I look forward to the day I can share my encounter with Mary Kwong and the first Chinese Lieutenant Governor of Alberta with my children and, hopefully my grandchildren.

Gardens of Hope

Edmonton, the city where I currently live, is divided into a north side and a south side by a breathtaking river valley (officially called the River Valley) that glows of auburn and gold in the fall and stands a majestic luscious green in the summer.

This River Valley stretches 7400 hectares with over 150 kilometres of trails to walk, bike, snowshoe or cross country ski, to name a few activities. The River Valley means a lot to me as I use it to train for my mountain climbing, or simply to walk through it to decompress after a hard day or week. I am very lucky to live close to it. Little did I know that our River Valley is more than an endless array of foliage, the legendary North Saskatchewan River, or our proud High Level Bridge. There is actually a hidden gem of a history about our River Valley, and the best person to tell me about it is Mr. Wei Wong.

Wei Wong was born in Edmonton in 1954, and he spent his early formative years in the Calder area. The Wong's first home was on the northwest corner of the family's market garden. The farm was about 20 acres and it was north of the train tracks on 127 Avenue and 113 Street, far away from Chinatown. A few years later, Wei and his family also gardened at the Beverly farm. To get there, you take 118 Avenue across to Edmonton's River Valley, turn right at the guard rail, and there is a plot of land on the east side of the bridge on the river flats. His father rented that land which was also 20 acres. The family farmed both the Calder and Beverly market gardens. "When I was a toddler, I basically worked at the farm. As soon as we could manage to stand up and walk, pulling weeds, tilling the soil, or whatever, we were made to work."

Around 1958, the Wong family moved from the Calder area to Dovercourt, which was also a suburb of the city of Edmonton. Wei's parents were isolated from their Chinese friends, as this property was also far from Chinatown. As a result, his family was not part of the main Chinese community.

Wei's parents ran their own market garden business with Wei's father as a market gardener. It was not a mainstream or popular Chinese community occupation. Did Wei's father's occupation as a market gardener shape Wei as a Chinese or Canadian person? "I think it did both. Like I said, as soon as I was able to stand up, we were made to work. This is different from the mainstream population. Because of the market garden, we had to work weekends, and the orders my father took, we had to deliver on Monday. Early Monday morning. If it was not harvest time, or if nothing was available, you had to be out there weeding and fixing things. And when the orders came in, we had to work Sundays until the orders were filled."

Me: That must have been hard with school work on top of the market gardening.

"We had to do our homework. The work ethic was, you come home; you finish your homework. Even on school days, during the busy season, my dad would come back home, pick us up and take us to the farm to work there too." "We never starved. We didn't have gourmet meals, but we didn't starve. The really interesting thing was that my father never took on another job in the winter as far as I know, since I was born. We just did our market garden in the summer, and when winter came, we just packed it in. He didn't take another job, which he had time to do, but he never did."

Wei's parents, Bark Ging Wong (father) and Young See Wong (mother), were born in Guangdong Province in China, in the district of Toishan. Bark Ging Wong came to Canada in 1921 when he was 13 years old with no education. The Chinese Exclusion Act became effective in 1923, and that law in itself prevented Wei's mother from coming to Canada until 1949. Wei's parents' ideals were - work hard but education came first. But Wei feels there was an unintended result. "They encouraged us to get an education so we wouldn't have to toil like they did. But in getting that education, they wanted us to excel and succeed, which we did, but the price is that we lost a lot of our Chinese. Even speaking. It's no different from a lot of immigrants today. Because we were away from Chinatown, it took a little more effort for my dad to buy things there and to socialize. In that aspect, we didn't learn as much about our culture as we could have. It's not like we lived in Chinatown and it was around us every day. We only celebrated some of the major festivities."

Was there extended family as Wei was growing up in Canada? Wei never knew his grandparents from either side, and he didn't have any aunts or uncles here either.

There have been family members who have married non-Chinese, but it was not an easy adjustment. Wei's adopted cousin-brother (Kwan) left Edmonton for England in 1968 on a university fellowship. He met a British young lady there. They married then moved back to Canada to establish a home. In regards to Wei's parents' reaction to Kwan's marriage to his British wife, they initially were not very happy about it but in time accepted it and adjusted to the reality. It did not help that interracial marriages were not readily accepted in the Chinese community back then. When it came time to communicate, there was a language barrier for his parents when they tried speaking with Kwan's wife. Wei's mother did not speak much English and his father knew some English because of his contact with the market garden customers, but it was limited. Regardless, a traditional tea ceremony was held at home and a large traditional Chinese wedding banquet was held at the Lychee Gardens Restaurant in their honour.

Did Wei's Chinese background influence his choice of a significant other? "I think it was expected. I knew my parents expected it because of the experience of my brother. But I didn't expect my kids to. They just found whoever they wanted." Both of Wei's daughters, Jasmine and Amber, married non-Chinese.

What were Wei's siblings' views on the Chinese culture? Kwan Wong (Wei's adopted cousin-brother) was born in China and came to Canada when he was 11. He has the highest education in the Wong family with a PhD from the University of Alberta in Biochemistry. Kwan is the first person from his Chinese village to obtain a PhD, and it was (and still is) a very proud achievement for his family. He became Associate Professor at Mount St. Vincent University in Halifax. Kwan is not as immersed in the Chinese culture because he moved away for university research for a long time. When he settled in Halifax to live, he was nowhere near a Chinatown.

Ging Wayne Wong was Wei's biological brother, who was 14 months older. Both Wayne and Wei went to school together with Wayne focussing on the sciences in university. He passed away in 1978. Lilly Mee Wong was Wei's biological sister. She was only 1 month old when she passed away. Lilly was the first Canadian-born in the Wong family.

Wei's parents wanted their kids to fit into mainstream society but also have their Chinese culture. They wanted their kids to experience both cultures. This preference differs from one family to another. In the early years, his parents wanted the kids to only speak Chinese. "When my brother went to Dovercourt School that first day for grade 1, at dismissal, they [the teachers] said 'go home, his English is not good enough. Come back next year'."

Growing up, Wei did feel a struggle with both the Canadian and Chinese cultures. When he was at home, he spoke Chinese to his parents. But as he went to school, he started losing more of his Chinese language. As he matured, he also started acting on behalf of his parents in terms of translation (i.e. filling out forms, banking, making appointments, etc.). They became dependent on him, and that was hard on Wei as a teenager. Now? He feels he has a balanced attitude towards both worlds even though he has lost most of his Chinese. "I think I can order a meal in a restaurant. Or, go to dim sum and order my favorite foods there. But I can't read it or write it, except for the numbers and my name." He speaks English to his wife Diane and to his kids.

However, Wei is very involved with Edmonton's Chinese (Mandarin) Bilingual program (his children graduated from the program). Even though he advocates the Mandarin program he feels there is still a disconnect because he never grew up speaking Mandarin nor does he speak it now. His family is from Toishan and spoke only Toishanese (which is closer to Cantonese than Mandarin). However, the Mandarin program curriculum taught something about the

Chinese culture. And the celebration of the Chinese culture, regardless of dialect, is something to be valued.

Growing up, fitting in was a challenge for Wei. In the Calder area, there was not as much racism because they were more isolated. Wei's parents had friends in the neighborhood and they were good friends. The Wong family rented some land from their Caucasian neighbors for their market garden. Unfortunately, the Wongs were one of only a few Chinese families in the Dovercourt area and this made them a target. In the 1960's, by the time Wei was in grade 6 or 7, there were only 3 Chinese families living in Dovercourt. During this difficult time, there was a lot of name calling, people climbing over the Wong's fence, or walking on their lawn. Wei's parents taught Wei and his siblings to ignore them and not to get into any fights. Now? Wei experiences racism very rarely. Wei feels we live in such a diverse city. If there was racism, it is more directed to new immigrants rather than the established immigrants who have been here for a long time. "I'm sure there still is, especially if you have poor English, you may be targeted. But as you can tell, I don't have much of an accent."

Despite the childhood challenges, Wei maintained some childhood best friends. Two of them were his best men at his wedding, and they are both non-Chinese. Most of Wei's childhood friends were Caucasian and he felt more comfortable around them. But he did not treat the Chinese kids any differently from his Caucasian friends.

Does Wei feel there is more or less acceptance for the Chinese culture today compared to the time he was growing up? He believes more so. "The population has increased so much. People realize now, well, not to brag, but the Chinese are good in math, good in the sciences, they are in the professions, and in the medical professions. All these breakthroughs and it's because they have a higher education. Education is still valued greatly amongst the Chinese. The work ethic is there. When my kids were in school, because our schools have the regular school program co-located with the Mandarin Bilingual program, a teacher who taught in the regular program wanted to teach the Chinese students because they were more well-behaved. The work ethic is looked upon as better than the mainstream."

When Wei was growing up, he remembers Chinese children who were put into weekend Chinese classes. These classes were outside of the main education structure. He recalls the Chinese children not liking these classes. They felt it took away from their play time. When the weather was so nice outside, all the children could think about was playing outdoors. But their parents forced them to learn Chinese for that extra couple of hours per week. With the current bilingual program, the children have to be in school anyways. For instance, in elementary school, the children receive 50% of their instruction in English and the other half in Chinese Mandarin. It is part of their school day, and it is not taking away from their play time. This system works better, as the kids are in school already and the bilingual program is built into their school day, not afterschool. Hooray for play time!

Interestingly enough, some of Wei's childhood Chinese education came from the Dreamland Theatre. Well, sort of. At this theatre, they had Chinese opera movies played in black and white. It used to be located straight down 97 Street on Jasper Ave where the Shaw Conference Centre is today. "Our parents, especially in the winter, dragged us there and made us sit through it." "This is what I remember ... you go there and there was all this candy and stuff in the front. You didn't have to pay for a ticket. There's a silver collection plate. I don't know if you know what that is?"

Me: No. Is it a collection of candies?

"No, it's a tray to collect donations. You throw in a dollar. Usually it's just change, back in the day. Then a lady or whomever has a pin, which has 3 colors of yarn on it. Once you made your donation, they pinned it on you, so they don't have to approach you again for donations. I remember these things. Then my parents would go in and we would watch a little bit and get bored ... not all this noise, the Chinese opera again! We would sneak out and buy some candies or something and wait for them. That was their time to socialize because they met their friends from out of town. They came in for these things from the surrounding restaurants whenever they had a day off."

Me: That was probably the only time they got to see each other. And then after that, go back to work.

With Wei and his family not living close to a Chinatown, without extended family around, his family's acceptance of interracial marriage and speaking less and less Chinese as he was growing up, his immersion into his post-secondary education also contributed to his loss of his Chinese culture. Equally important, there were only a few Chinese people employed during his career in the aviation industry. His occupation as a Flight Service Specialist in Canada's remote Arctic also contributed to this culture loss. Many of the Chinese are in the hard sciences or medicine, not aviation. There are more today, but during Wei's career there were not many Chinese people working in the aviation industry in Canada.

Despite Wei losing much of his Chinese culture, he is currently quite involved with the Edmonton Chinese Bilingual Education Association, but more so when his children were in the program. Attending Chinese New Year's celebrations and going for dim sum are also some of Wei's activities in the Chinese community. He is also involved in posting Chinese events that are happening around the city onto the web, such as Asian Heritage Month or Chinese New Year celebrations. He has also been taking his eldest granddaughter, Ella, to Chinese drumming classes. At the time, she was in kindergarten. But it has also been quality time spent together as grandfather and granddaughter. "When she was a baby, we took her to Chinese New

Year's celebrations; she was always fascinated with the lions and the drumming. So I thought, ok, if you're interested ..." Does Wei identify with all or some of the Chinese cultural lifestyle? Some. He has 2 cultures now and "I take the best of both cultures."

Has Wei ever been to China? No. "There's a reason why people left China."

Me: If you were given the opportunity to visit, would you?

"I would. Just like any vacation planning, I suppose. But I have no urge. But my brother (Kwan) did. He went back to search for our ancestral village. The village where my father basically was born. He went back to the village of Chew Ging and found remnants of the house. Because he (Kwan) still has his brother living in Hong Kong, he was able to take him there. They hired a taxi to go there. He knows where it is. Carmen, my niece, has also been there. But I haven't. I would like to know where it is. In fact, I've done some research of the family tree and try to write up a bit of each person's history. Slowly, it's just a hobby."

Wei does not believe in choosing his physician, accountant or dentist just because they are Chinese. "You know, there's some thought there. Some people, who are in the Chinese community, would patronize the Chinese doctor, Chinese lawyer, or pharmacist. But because we grew up here, it probably doesn't make a difference. There are two trains of thought. If you want to go to a Chinese, are they the most qualified? Just because they're Chinese ... like the [civic] election, some people said 'vote these Chinese people in'. Why? Are they even qualified? They're running for the first time and have no experience." "The doctor we went to was Jewish and he was our family doctor for our entire lives. Through my dad, and us, and even through our kids, until he retired. Same doctor. He made house calls back then."

Is Wei more proud to be Chinese, Canadian or both? "I would say both. I think as a kid, we wanted to fit in. You can't change your appearance, right? And really, at the time, I wanted to be part of mainstream society and not get discriminated against or get called names. You try to become as 'white' as possible. But now? I want to retain our identity. We are Chinese and you can't hide that fact and so we are Chinese Canadian as well. We contributed to Canadian society and now the focus for me is like this: the Chinese population is increasing and it's beneficial to have more people learn Chinese so that's why I'm an advocate for the Chinese Bilingual program and promote understanding through culture as well as education. A lot of the Chinese history is unknown to the mainstream. I like to read Chinese authors too. Asian authors. Preferably the Canadian ones."

Has Wei ever been asked "No, Really, Where Are You From?" "I have been. I don't get offended by it because they don't know any better. But at the same time, they are assuming that just because you look different, that you're from another country. So these people are not realizing that Canada has a population that comes from everywhere, everywhere around the world. And I suppose for them to ask you that question, they want to get to know you? Like I said, I'm not offended by it; they don't know where you come from and they're showing their interest."

I started writing Wei's chapter with the intention of focussing on his family's market garden and its place in Edmonton's history, but something shifted for me. Do not get me wrong. Wei's family history is still fascinating and it will always have a special place in Edmonton's history. When I visit the River Valley today, I still think about the Wong's market garden property and the long hours the family endured working on it. What has transpired for me as I learned more about Wei is that the gardens his parents toiled on and worked their hands to the bone at represented the sacrifices they made and the resiliency they possessed in trying to raise a family in a foreign land. The market gardens were gardens of hope. A legacy of a different sort. It was not a legacy of passing down money or personal property, but a legacy of passing down hope and their hard work ethic values. They were gardens of hope for their children and future generations to have a better life in the new country, a hope for a more secure future in Canada, a hope that the future generations would not have to work as hard as they did, as they planted and harvested their vegetable gardens day after day, week after week, year after year. And it has paid off. All of Wei's siblings and their families have done so well in Canada, including Wei. Wei, being first-generation Canadian-born, father of three, is now a grandfather to five beautiful and healthy third-generation Canadian-born grandchildren.

Finding Michelle

"You have to read this," my friend Susan said to me as she handed me an article from a local travel magazine. "You'll like it—it's about a Chinese family that lives in a small town."

So I read the article and thoroughly enjoyed it. And even though I put the article aside, I was still digesting everything I had read. And I wondered about the possibility of interviewing Michelle J. Wong, the author of the article, for my book. I must admit, however, that I held out little hope that she would agree to it—I mean, she's a film producer, and a very accomplished one at that. Why would she want to talk to me?

Besides, the article didn't provide any contact information for Michelle.

Eventually, I realized that I was just making excuses. What was the worst that could happen if I asked her for an interview? And as far as getting in touch with her... well... I did have Google at my disposal.

So I jumped into the task of finding Michelle. And Google came through for me: there, I found an email address. Of course, I had no way of knowing if this was the right "Michelle Wong," but I sent a message anyway. And, lo and behold, within a short time, Michelle responded—yes, I had the right Michelle. And, yes, she would be happy to sit down and talk to me. Hallelujah for technology!

By the time I interviewed Michelle, I had already interviewed seven other people. And each and every one of my subject's stories amazed and intrigued me. Michelle's story is no different.

Michelle J. Wong was born and raised 145 miles northeast of Edmonton, Alberta, in the small town of St. Paul. When Michelle was growing up there (from the 1960s to the 1980s), the population of St. Paul was somewhere between 3,500 and 4,000. A full half of the population is French-Canadian, not surprising for a town that was founded by a Catholic priest (Father Lacombe). The other half of the population is approximately two-thirds Ukrainian and one-third First Nations. And then, of course, there is a smattering of other visible minorities.

Michelle's parents were born in Guangzhou, which is in the southern part of China in the 'sei (four) yap' counties. They both grew up in that same area, but in separate villages that were less than ten miles apart.

Michelle's paternal grandfather immigrated to Canada in the 1920s and travelled throughout western Canada, eventually putting down roots in St. Paul. In 1947, he brought his family, including Michelle's father who was 18 at the time, over to Canada to join him.

When he was in his mid-twenties, Michelle's father contracted tuberculosis and was bedridden for a few years. But as soon as he recovered, his father sent him to Hong Kong to find a wife. Eventually, he narrowed it down to two women, at which point he consulted with his aunts and uncles. They told him to pick the woman who was physically stronger and able to work harder. So it was through that advice that Michelle's mother and father were married. Immediately following the wedding, the couple boarded a ship to Canada to begin their new life together.

As it turned out, it was not the kind of life that Michelle's mother, who was 19 at the time, had been expecting. Before the wedding, Michelle's father had told her mother that he had a house and a restaurant waiting for them in Canada, and to her, this signaled "city." When the couple landed in Victoria, British Columbia, Michelle's mother was hopeful; she liked Victoria. Then they travelled on to Vancouver, and she liked Vancouver even more. She hoped that the port city of Vancouver, which reminded her in many ways of Hong Kong, would be the place where they would hang their hats and get about the business of this "new life."

But it was not to be. Instead, they boarded a train headed for the Prairies. The train stopped in Edmonton, Alberta. Not a port city, but a city nonetheless. But the trip didn't end in Edmonton either. The couple got into a car and kept moving—eventually stopping further northeast of Edmonton, in the landlocked town of St. Paul.

By this time, Michelle's mother's perception of her new husband had changed substantially. The glamorous picture she had had in her head of an overseas man who lived in a port city was replaced by a picture of someone very much like a farmer, who lived in the middle of nowhere, where there was not another Chinese person in sight (beyond Michelle's father's family). Michelle's mother spent the majority of her marriage trying to coax Michelle's father to move somewhere with a Chinese community.

But Michelle's father always had a reason not to grant his wife's request: the children were too young, he had an obligation to his parents, and he needed to run the restaurant. Maybe later, he would say. Finally, when Michelle was in high school, her mother asked, for the last time, if Michelle's father would consider moving. He said no, and Michelle's mother realized at that point that he had never had any intention of ever leaving St. Paul. After 20 years, Michelle's mother had had enough: she moved away and left her family in St. Paul.

But of course, Michelle points out, there are two sides to every story. From Michelle's father's perspective, he needed to stay in St. Paul. As the oldest son, he had an obligation to his parents: it was his responsibility to take care of them. And he had built a restaurant, a successful business, in St. Paul. He wasn't about to uproot and leave everything—his whole life was in that small town.

And owning a restaurant was no small thing: not every Chinese family could afford to open one. But in the early 1950s, Michelle's grandfather had entered into a partnership with one or two other immigrants (none of them were rich enough to open one on their own), and the dream of owning a restaurant became a reality.

Michelle tells me why her grandfather had picked St. Paul to settle and begin his life as a restaurant owner.

"He told me that it was a simple matter of St. Paul not having a Chinese restaurant. Edmonton was too saturated, and most other small towns already had at least one Chinese restaurant by then, but St. Paul didn't. So it was a logical choice."

In the mid-1960s, Michelle's father opened a second restaurant, the Boston Café, and it was here that Michelle found her cultural perspective. Like most Chinese restaurants in Canadian small towns, the Boston Café served Chinese-Canadian cuisine. During the day, the clientele was predominantly Caucasian, and then, later in the afternoon and into the evening, more First Nations customers would come in.

"The restaurant," Michelle tells me, "was our 'safe space.' People came in to eat the food, but they also got to know us as people because we would chit-chat with them."

"So they also got to know about the Chinese culture?" I ask.

"Absolutely," she says. "Even though it was a certain version of it. Obviously my serving people food and sitting and chatting with them didn't give them the same perspective as they would have gotten had they gone behind the kitchen doors where all the screaming and stuff goes on. But it was better than nothing."

The family business shaped Michelle's childhood in profound ways. As soon as she and her siblings were old enough to participate in running the restaurant, they spent most of their time there.

"I started working in the restaurant when I was five or six years old," Michelle tells me. "All of us kids started working when we were really young, but in subtle ways. Not like a "job" job. Mostly I just took commands: I peeled carrots or other vegetables, washed dishes, stuff like that. When I got older and taller and could reach more things, I moved on to taking orders, waitressing, stocking shelves, stocking the freezer."

I ask Michelle why she never rebelled against the work.

"Participating in the restaurant was sort of the same as participating in the family," Michelle explains, "so it gave me a sense of purpose as well. As a Chinese daughter, it was my job to help in whatever way I could. And that made me feel like I was important to the family."

Michelle also tells me that she believes that having worked in the restaurant from such a young age is part of the reason she is now a very task-oriented person.

"If you give me an order," she says, "I can fill it really quickly. My grandmother was like Chef Ramsey, and I was like a sous chef. To my grandmother, there was nothing good about idle hands. So even now I'm always doing something. Recycling, doing dishes, straightening things, whatever. I have a really strong work ethic because of it, and I think that's a good thing, not a bad thing."

But there was a tradeoff as well: Michelle had little spare time as a child.

"I remember not having holidays as a kid," she tells me. "And not having evenings or weekends free like other kids did. I remember being amazed that people actually took summer holidays. It was hard for me to comprehend how other people couldn't be working all the time like I was."

In some ways, Michelle's parents were the complete opposite of a lot of typical Chinese parents who push their children to be doctors or engineers. For Michelle, there was no pressure to do anything any more complicated than working in the restaurant. Women usually aren't expected to do anything more than take care of others. This is also part of the reason Michelle's parents never pushed education on her or her sister (although they did push it more on the one boy, Phillip). But there are other reasons as well that education didn't hold all that much value for Michelle's parents.

Michelle's mother had a pretty bleak view of education because her father (Michelle's grandfather) had gone to school and, as a result, hardly ever engaged in physical labour. Michelle's mother felt that going to school was a bad thing: it made people lazy. Her attitude was that when you're in school, you're just sitting. Yes, you're using your head, but you're not actually doing anything. For the longest time, education was irrelevant to Michelle's mother.

As for Michelle's father, he had only a high school education, and he was very successful, so he didn't really see why an education was even necessary.

Michelle attended Glen Avon, a Protestant elementary school, in which Ukrainians, a very small group of Chinese (Michelle included), and a couple of other ethnicities made up the cultural components of the school. For high school, the Catholic and Protestant schools combined into one (Regional High). This is when the rich French-Canadian heritage of St. Paul and the French-Canadian culture became much more apparent to Michelle.

The only "Chinese" education Michelle received was in her Social Studies class. Unfortunately, Michelle tells me, Chinese stereotypes, either in textbooks or in the minds of her peers, predominated. For example, Michelle remembers drawing a picture of a Chinese man on a title page for an assignment. In her rendering, the man was given both buckteeth and slanted eyes.

China was also, according to the curriculum at the time, a "sleeping giant." So that was the only picture Michelle had of Communist China. Her knowledge of China and the Chinese culture never went beyond that.

As an adult, however, Michelle received a very different kind of Chinese education. She tells me that her work as a documentary filmmaker was a vital tool for her to deconstruct her feelings about being Chinese and to help her understand herself more as a Chinese person. But we will talk more about Michelle's filmmaking in a moment.

So how did Michelle maintain her Chinese culture growing up under these conditions? In answer to that question, Michelle points to language.

"We spoke Chinese (Toishan dialect) when I was growing up," she says. "When we were kids, our mother was always yelling at us to speak Chinese. And we were always wondering why—but I realized later that it was because if we lost the language, we wouldn't be able to communicate with her anymore. She spoke very little English, so she had to keep us talking in Chinese."

Michelle still speaks the language and is able to use it in Chinatown if need be. She tells me that she's glad she has retained the language. She may not be at adult level vocabulary wise, she says, but it's "good enough." And, of course, she still speaks Chinese with her parents.

The presence of extended family was prominent throughout Michelle's childhood. Michelle tells me that she feels fortunate to have had her grandparents in her life when she was young.

"I was lucky to have them," she says, "and I was also lucky that I got to know them so well. Because we worked together everyday, I got to know them even better than I would have otherwise. And that also played a big part in me feeling like I was important and part of the family."

Michelle also has an aunt (her father's sister) who lived in St. Paul when Michelle was young, although that aunt has since moved to Edmonton. And Michelle also had numerous family members in Edmonton, whom Michelle visited often. They also spent time visiting other Chinese families (most of whom also owned restaurants) in other small Alberta towns, such as Bonnyville.

Besides the Wongs, there was only one other Chinese family living in St. Paul when Michelle was growing up. The father of that family (we will call him "Mr. X") was a man Michelle's grandfather met on the boat coming to Canada. Eventually, this man would also become a partner in the restaurant business. There were plans at one point for Michelle's grandfather and Mr. X to open a laundromat together, but they had a falling out, which soon took the shape of a family feud that was passed down to Michelle's father. As a result of the feud, Michelle was instructed not to interact with Mr. X's family. This was a bit awkward, because Michelle's grandfather and Mr. X had actually bought houses side-by-side.

Michelle likened the feud to Fred Flintstone and Barney Rubble having a fight, and Betty and Wilma being forbidden to speak to one another. As for Michelle, she did have some interactions with the X family, but those interactions were minimal. She knew their names, and sometimes participated in activities where a member of the X family happened to be participating as well, but the Wongs and the Xs certainly didn't ever get together to celebrate Christmas or the Chinese New Year. At best, the two families were like distant acquaintances.

So what did Michelle do to "fit in" growing up in St. Paul?

"I tried to fit in in different ways," she says. "I became the class clown for one thing. I had a good sense of humour, and in the yearbook, I'm shown as the person voted as the funniest person in my class. I think humour was a way for me to sort of disappear. I was fat, or at least larger, as a child. So humour helped me avoid any big issues—like dating. I was friends with everyone, but never in a "sexual object" kind of a way and that was something I think I unconsciously created for myself."

At home, Michelle tells me, she was the Chinese version of herself, while away from home and the restaurant, she was a regular, integrated Canadian kid. But being integrated didn't mean that she was immune from teasing concerning her ethnicity and her weight.

Michelle was subjected to a lot of name-calling when she was growing up, but the abuse rarely went any further than that. She does, however, remember a much more violent event involving her brother, Phillip. When Phillip was young, a group of boys in a park beat him up for no other reason than that he was Chinese. When Phillip walked into the restaurant with his face bloodied, beaten, and swollen, Michelle's mother was shocked, and she asked him what had happened. Angered by Phillip's story, she, along with Phillip, left the restaurant and set out to confront the boys responsible. When they got to the park, Phillip pointed out the group of boys, and Michelle's mother picked up a two-by-four piece of plywood, made a beeline for them, and proceeded to hit them in the legs with the plywood.

Michelle tells me that she will never forget how tough her mom was that day, and how proud she is that her mother was a powerful woman who wasn't afraid of anyone or anything, unlike many Chinese women who don't want to cause trouble or say anything and just hope that the problem will go away.

As far as the Wong family and the restaurant go, episodes of discrimination never went beyond racial slurs, and those generally came from people who were unfamiliar to the Wong family. As an example, Michelle tells me that from time to time a baseball team would come in, and when they were calling for a waitress, they would say things like "Yo, chop suey!" or "Chop suey!" or "Chop chop!"

But most of the customers (60-70 percent) who came into the restaurant were regulars who knew the Wongs and had a good relationship with them. Those customers, Michelle tells me, wouldn't have even considered saying such things.

The clientele of the restaurant consisted of primarily Caucasians and First Nations. Michelle had, and has, a special fondness for the First Nations.

"I had the chance to really get to know a lot of (First Nations) people," she tells me. "And I always thought it was cool to have had that extra cultural influence in my life. My experience is that they're extremely friendly, very kind people. I know they get stereotyped as well, just like the Chinese or any other group, but the whole thing about them being drunks and stumbling around is just that—a stereotype. When I go to a casino and see a group of (First Nations) people, it warms my heart because I know that chances are that they are very much like the people I grew up around.

"Once you walked into our restaurant," Michelle continues, "you were equal to everyone else there. There was never anyone who was considered better, or worse, than anyone else. And that's the way it should be everywhere."

But, even for all that equality, Michelle would eventually learn about the gender divide in Chinese culture. When she was 14, Michelle asked her father if she could run the family business when she grew up. His answer: a firm "no." This surprised Michelle because not only had she always seen herself as her father's "favourite," but also because she knew that neither her brother nor her sister had any interest in the family business.

"My father wanted my brother to run it for sure," Michelle tells me. "But my brother wasn't at all interested in staying in St. Paul. So I couldn't really understand why he would say 'no.' And it was disappointing for sure. I felt rejected."

For probably the first time in her life, Michelle really reflected on what it meant to be female in Chinese culture.

"It gave me a really strong sense of the gender aspect of our family," she tells me. "It's like… you're a Chinese female, so for sure you're cooking and cleaning. And there were things my mom would make sure I did that my brother never had to do. And I remember wondering why he didn't have to do the laundry, why he didn't have to do the dishes."

Michelle goes on to tell me that while she did notice some of this while she was young, she generally figured the division of labour simply had something to do with them being children. But eventually, there was no denying the strong sense of gender roles and the different expectations for each gender that permeated their lives and culture.

"My mom," Michelle says, "was always making sure that I could do all these things because if I were to get married, which of course I was expected to do, then I had to know how to do all this stuff."

"She was preparing you for marriage?" I ask.

"Yes," Michelle says. "Even though she didn't say it, and even though, in my own mind, I knew about my own sense of sexual identity. I knew that these Chinese cultural ideals didn't quite fit with the future I saw for myself, but at the same time I felt like the Chinese culture had already sealed my fate—without my input or permission."

But Michelle also had bigger issues than culture to contend with. Besides being Chinese, Michelle is also a lesbian.

"I would say that I actually struggled less with culture than I did with sexuality. That was more of a struggle for me. And if you look at my body of work, you can see that I have the "Chinese" work and then the "sexual identity" work. Those were two things I was trying to reconcile into one."

But, ultimately, Michelle would find her own way despite the pressures, uncertainties, and disappointments.

"In retrospect," she says, "I look back at it all, and I think it all worked out for the better anyway. It forced me to go out into the world and carve out a career for myself outside of the restaurant. And a life for myself outside of the expectations that were put on me."

At 18, Michelle moved to Edmonton to attend the University of Alberta, where she studied in the Education program, with a major in Drama and a minor in English. She had always been interested in the Arts, museums, and education, and she chose drama because she hoped, eventually, to get into film and television. The Arts, and Fine Arts in particular, have always been a non traditional educational route in the Chinese community (there were only one or two Chinese students besides Michelle in any of her classes), but Michelle knew what she wanted and was determined to pursue her goals.

When Michelle finished her Bachelor's degree, she was given the opportunity to complete her Master's degree in Playwriting, but she found that she had a knack for teaching. Instead of pursuing her Master's, she got her permanent teaching certificate and spent three years teaching before going into filmmaking.

When Michelle pursued filmmaking, her mother wasn't exactly thrilled with her decision.

"My mom kept asking me, 'What are you doing? What's filmmaking?'" Michelle says. "She saw it as nothing more than me playing or fooling around with something. When I raised eighty thousand dollars to make Return Home (Michelle's first documentary), she kept asking me why I wasn't using the money to buy a house. Of course, she didn't understand that the money had been earmarked for a film, and I couldn't just do anything I wanted with it."

On the other hand, Michelle's parents never tried to "forbid" her to do anything.

"I never felt like there was any strong support for anything I did," she says, "but they also never told me I couldn't do it."

So Michelle went ahead and did what she wanted to do, which was to make a documentary about her family. As part of the process of putting the documentary together, she interviewed her grandparents about their arranged marriage and their wedding day. She asked each of them what they thought and felt about the whole concept of arranged marriage.

In response to the question, Michelle's grandmother told her that a Chinese woman must be dedicated first to her father, then to her husband, and, finally, to her son. This is a Chinese woman's fate — whether she likes it or not. Marriage, as Michelle's grandfather described it, is like a left hand and right hand: the female is the left hand and the male is the right. And you must put them together to get things done because you need two hands to do anything. Marriage, he said, has nothing to do with love. Marriage is just a necessity, a way to live, another step in life. Prior to their own marriage, Michelle's grandparents had never met, or even seen, one another. They were simply brought together by a local matchmaker as was the tradition in those days.

Michelle then asked her grandparents if they loved each other or if they even liked each other once they were married. In answer to that question, they both simply chuckled. To them, the issue of love was irrelevant: it's not love, but hard work and tenacity that put food in one's stomach. The families and the village approved the match, knowing how solid each family clan was. And Michelle's grandparents never contested it: they were both okay with the arrangements that were made on their behalves because both of their families would benefit.

Michelle's older sister was the first in the Wong family to marry a non Chinese person. This caused a bit of confusion as far as tradition goes: in a Caucasian wedding, it's traditional for the bride's family to pay for the wedding, and in a Chinese wedding, it's traditional for the groom's family to pay. To avoid any confusion over this issue, Michelle's sister and her husband-to-be simply avoided the traditional "big circus" wedding. Instead, they went to a justice of the peace.

I ask Michelle about her family's reaction to these events, and she tells me that going to a justice of the peace was actually a good idea in that it avoided any cultural clashes. On the other hand, she says, there was a reaction, but it had more to do with the couple not having a big wedding than it did with any cultural issues.

I ask Michelle what her mother's perception of her new son-in-law (Brian) was. In many ways, Michelle tells me, her mom feels like she has "won the lottery" with Brian.

"He's a great guy," Michelle says, "and very traditional. He prefers for the woman to stay home and take care of the house and kids while he brings home the money. My mom loves that about him. And she knows he can be trusted—that he's faithful, and he'll take care of things.

"I'm sure," Michelle continues, "that, early on, my mom really wanted my sister to marry Chinese. She even had my sister move to Vancouver for a year, when my sister was 18, to see if she could find a Chinese guy she liked. But my sister hated it in Vancouver. And when it was clear to my mom that my sister wasn't going to marry Chinese, she let go of the idea and embraced Brian because he's a wonderful man for her daughter."

Michelle's brother Phillip, on the other hand, married a Taiwanese woman. But Michelle's aunt on her father's side has four daughters, and of those four, three married Caucasian men. And Michelle's aunt on her mother's side has two children: one who is single and one who is married to a Canadian-born Chinese man. Clearly, there are no hard, fast rules about whom one can marry in the Wong family.

Still, Michelle feels that her cultural experiences growing up in a small town had a definite impact on her selection of a significant other, but not, perhaps, in the way one would think.

"I couldn't imagine kissing a Chinese girl." Michelle tells me "It would be like... well... kissing my sister. And it's not that I don't find Chinese women attractive, it's just that I never really saw the possibility of another Chinese person being the right partner for me. Probably because I never had any Chinese friends growing up, unless I was related to them. I mean, it's not like I'm attracted, in that way, to Caucasian people exclusively, although my partner happens to be Caucasian. I have also been attracted to Southeast Asian women and to (First Nations) women. Just never to Chinese women. There just weren't any Chinese women to be attracted to growing up in St. Paul, so I guess I sort of excluded that as a possibility."

The Chinese culture, Michelle tells me, is reflected very differently in her siblings' lives than it is in hers. Her older sister, who is now a housewife, knows more than Michelle does about the pressures and positioning of both cultures. And Phillip, as the only son, experienced the pressures and expectations that came with that. It was particularly difficult, Michelle says, for him to meet all the obligations that were put on him. And his inability to live up to those expectations even resulted in a falling out with his father.

"My parents expected Phillip to be something 'more' than us girls, and something different than what he actually was," Michelle says. "So there was a lot of pressure on him. He went to university for two and a half years, and he tried really hard to live up to his position as the 'golden child,' but it just wasn't working out for him. By the time I started university, he was dropping out. So he left school and went to join my mom."

Michelle's sister currently lives in Pasadena, California, which is a predominately Caucasian area of Los Angeles. That, Michelle tells me, is where her sister is comfortable, having grown up around Caucasians.

"She doesn't even really feel comfortable around Mexican people," Michelle says, "just Caucasians."

Oddly enough, it's Brian who would like to move the family to an area with more Chinese people, based mostly on the strength of the public school system in the Chinese area. But Michelle's sister flatly refuses.

Of course, given Michelle's education and occupation, she has had more opportunities than her siblings to explore her cultural identity. In the early 1990s, when Michelle was 25, she was introduced to feminism, cultural heritage, and race relations, which were popular topics with the National Film Board at the time. Exploring all of these concepts helped Michelle negotiate her issues.

"I'm Chinese, I'm a woman, and I'm a lesbian," she says. "But I've never been denied a job or anything like that because of it. I'm all of those things, but I've never let it hold me back from doing what I want to do. And I refuse to fall into the stereotypes.

"If you get to know who I am as a person," Michelle continues, "and then I tell you I'm gay, you'll just go, 'Oh, wow, okay—so Michelle's a lesbian, but she's so normal.' And I think that's it—it's a matter of getting to know me as a person. Yes, I'm Chinese, and a woman, and gay, but I don't push from one or the other of those things. It's a whole package kind of a deal. And that's how I break the stereotypes. I'm Chinese, but I may not be that version of Chinese that you're thinking about. Or that version of a woman. Or that version of a lesbian. And I'm not a token anything—I'm just the sum of the parts that make me a total person."

But Michelle didn't come to these conclusions overnight or in isolation. She needed a little push along the way. For Michelle, that "push" came when she was part of a team working on a human affairs television show and was invited to Toronto to participate in a professional development session.

"There were a variety of ethnicities represented there," Michelle tells me. "There was an Aboriginal person, a Chinese person (Michelle), an African person, a Southeast Asian person, etc. And I stood up in front of them all and said, 'As a Chinese woman, I'm really grateful for this opportunity to try to tell you the stories of my culture.' And Rita (Rita Deverell, a pioneer in television who was working at Vision TV at the time) stopped me. She said, 'Just hang on, Michelle. Just so you know, I know you're Chinese, and I know you're a woman, but I also want you to know that you don't have to feel obligated to tell those stories. I didn't hire you because you're Chinese, because you're gay, or because you're a woman. I hired you because I found you to be an interesting person, and you just happen to bring all those things with you as part of the package.

"That," Michelle says, "really opened my mind because I was used to being with the film board, where they were pretty much telling me, 'You're these things, and you have an obligation to represent your culture.' And then Rita comes in and just bashes it open and says, 'Yeah, but you're so much more than just that.'"

Still, Michelle has had to contend with the odd racist encounter as an adult. She remembers particularly one event that took place during her first year of teaching in Slave Lake, Alberta.

"I remember coming out of a 7-Eleven," she tells me, "and there were a couple of young kids standing outside the door. They started chanting 'Chinky Chinky Chinaman.' I remember being really surprised and thinking, 'Oh my God! I'm an adult, and it's the same shit as when I was a kid!'"

But, Michelle tells me, that incidence didn't have the same negative effect on her as it would have when she was child. Those words, she says, hold no power over her now and only reveal the ignorance of the people speaking them. By dissecting and analyzing her thoughts about these kinds of incidents, she says, she was able to disarm their power over her.

"There's a process of 'internalized racism,'" Michelle says. "You are educated with the same beliefs as everyone else, so they're within you. So when someone says, 'You fuckin' chink!' the part of you that believes the negative connotations behind the words is hurt, frustrated, angry. But once you realize the emptiness and misconceptions behind those words, you can render them powerless. Now, if someone says something like that, I just tell them they don't know what they're talking about. It doesn't have that same negative effect on me because I've dealt with those buttons within me."

Michelle tells me that she also remembers arguing with a panhandler outside of a library once.

"He kept saying that he was born here," Michelle says, "as if I wasn't. He said that my parents were immigrants and should go back where they belong—as if someone in his background didn't also have to immigrate to Canada in order for him to be standing there.

"That was the first time that I actually spoke back instead of walking away. It was the first time I ever really stood up for myself. Before, I would have just walked past him, but that time I felt like my pride was at stake."

That incident, Michelle says, gave her courage. As a Chinese woman, talking back was new to her. As with most Chinese women, Michelle was raised to not talk back or rock the boat—a woman couldn't possibly have the ability to really think things through or to question things. In the traditional Chinese culture, this is a matter of respect and knowing one's place in the hierarchy. The role of the woman is to accept things and, most importantly, to obey the man. The man, as the protector, is allowed to talk back, but the woman must simply suppress the anger and carry it with her. But this, as Michelle points out, is both dangerous and unhealthy. So now, she says, she doesn't always stay silent. And if someone calls her a 'fuckin' chink,' she doesn't let it tear her apart inside.

This is not to say, however, that Michelle never experiences the push and pull between eastern and western philosophies and all that that entails. Western culture promotes individualism: it's all about what you want and how you get it. Eastern culture, on the other hand, is all about the clan or the community. There is no concept of the singular: if you make sacrifices, it's for the good of the family. If you bring shame to yourself, you bring shame to the family. If are successful, you share that success, and the credit for it, with the family. These are two extreme ends of a pendulum that swings between a "me-

me" attitude and a "we-we" attitude. Michelle explains what it's like for her to juggle these two extremes.

"You've got to live with one foot in each world," she says, "where you want personal satisfaction and achievement, yet you want to be a good daughter, a good family member—unselfish, self-sacrificing, humble, modest, all those things. Trying to balance all of that can be really hard at times, and I'm still figuring out how to do it."

For Michelle, this balancing act is eased by telling stories. "But the main reason I do 'personal' story documentaries is because no one can dispute my personal experiences. They may not want to believe me, but they're still my experiences."

Michelle then goes on to explain to me why she believes it's necessary to share personal experiences if the audience is to relate to the filmmaker— or writer, as the case may be. To demonstrate, she draws two intersecting lines, forming an upside down cone shape. Each line, she tells me, represents the "general" information, and they eventually merge to "specific" information. The idea, she says, is to dig deeper and deeper, revealing more and more specific details. And it may initially be uncomfortable for the audience or it may come across as narcissistic, but eventually the two lines will form a huge "X," and the bottom half will open up. This, Michelle says, is where the specific becomes the universal—where a specific event in the storyteller's life becomes the representation of a universal theme: family, love, loss, struggle, crisis, or whatever. So it is through that that the person hearing the story can relate to the events: although all of our stories are different, we can all identify with those universal themes. And someone may even recognize themselves in some of the specific details as well. For instance, Michelle told me that her older sister experienced anxiety when she was around Chinese people. And I told Michelle that I often felt the same way, but never before had I realized that I wasn't alone in that.

But back to the topic of culture. I ask Michelle what role her education and occupation play in her maintaining, or not maintaining, her Chinese identity.

"Well," she says, "going into the Arts is a pretty unChinese thing to do, and there aren't a whole lot of successful Asian artists to look to. So I try to be that for others. Like when I go to universities to speak, I'm the proof that you can be Chinese and have a career in the Arts. There weren't a whole lot of role models for me though, and even now, there's only a handful of us.

"So I don't find a lot of reinforcement of my culture in my career. If you look at screen credits, my name is one of the few that isn't Caucasian. So it's important to me to be that role model for others."

And Michelle takes this role seriously. She is active as a mentor to other Asian people working in the Arts.

Today, when Michelle tells her mother how much she makes as a producer, her mother backs off—it's finally clear to her mother that she isn't just playing around. But it's still hard for Michelle's mother to let go of some of those old expectations.

"She still wants me to be 'taken care of,'" Michelle says. "Once you're married, it's like they (parents) don't have to worry about you anymore—they can let go. But for me, because I'm a lesbian and there's no guy showing up, I think my mom held onto that concern for me a lot longer than she needed to."

Michelle tells me that she has a friend who is currently struggling with these same Chinese cultural expectations around the issue of marriage. One day, her friend was talking to her brother about their mother's will, and Michelle's friend came to find out that she was not named in the will. In other words, Michelle's friend would get nothing—everything would go to the one boy in the family. According to traditional Chinese culture, Michelle's friend is expected to get married and be taken care of by someone else. The modern day Chinese ideology would think otherwise. The traditional Chinese mentality believes inheritance is strictly for the boy in the family because he is expected to continue the lineage and take care of his parents in their old age. Also because Michelle's friend is gay and won't ever be married to a man, this paints her as a 'failure' or 'deviant' in the traditional Chinese cultural terms.

So once again we see traditional Chinese culture dictating the path an individual must take, attempting to seal the fate for both Chinese women and men, in the process. In this case, Michelle's friend's brother already has a great job, yet he receives money from his parents to buy new furniture, or even a new home. According to Michelle, it's highly unlikely that her friend's brother will tell their mother that the arrangement is unfair. So the likelihood is that, when all is said and done, Michelle's friend will be left out in the cold. It's a tradition that has been passed down for thousands of years, and whether or not it can ever be changed depends on so many factors in each individual's life, such as family dynamics and whether or not members of the family can talk openly about such things. But even then, there is no guarantee that a sibling is going to be "fair" when the time comes. Not exclusive to the Chinese culture, the inheritance principle that favors the Chinese male offspring, also exists in other cultures.

Michelle has visited the land where all these traditions originate. She travelled to China with her mother and stepfather. Michelle tells me that she found China interesting, and would like to go back and see more of the country.

It's so poor in China, Michelle says, and there are so many people that if you were to live there, your windows of opportunity would shrink by leaps and bounds as you age. You are really only "good" for anything between the ages of 16 and 23, and then you are pretty much left to your own devices. And there isn't much in China for someone without an education (and women must rely mostly on their looks).

And even if you work hard, it probably won't get you very far. As an example, Michelle tells me that a two hour massage in China costs 30 Chinese Yuan, which equates to approximately eight or nine dollars. In Canada, it's unheard of for a masseuse to be paid so little. But we must keep in mind that their lower hourly wages and salaries are due to the lower cost of living in China, in comparison to Canada's higher cost of living. As Canadians, we may find it next to impossible to have three meals a day for under $10.00, but it would be possible in China.

"When you're around that kind of poverty, you realize the opportunities you have. I was thinking about my grandparents coming over and what it meant, and the sacrifices they made so that I could have the life I have, and all of this," Michelle says as she sweeps her arm through the air to encompass her home and everything in it. "People can romanticize all they want about the exotic and mysterious Orient, but realistically, the opportunities for a better life just aren't there."

While she was in China, Michelle shot nine hours of footage that follows her mother's journey. Together, they went to the house her mother grew up in, which had changed so much, Michelle says, that it broke her mother's heart. Her mother remembered it being new and modern, but when she returned, it seemed so dirty and run down.

"My mom left China when she was 19," Michelle says, "so it had been 50 year since she'd last been there. It really changed the romanticized version she had in her head," Michelle says. "She was able to release all of that because she actually went back and saw the reality. It was like closure for her.

"Later, when we were travelling back to the airport, I asked her if she missed it, and she told me that she was glad that she left—that she probably would have ended up being a farm girl or a worker in a shop had she stayed. 'I wouldn't have much of life,' she said, 'but now I have a house in the States (where she now lives), a car, a pension, my own life. I have comforts.'"

So Michelle's mother has gone from China, to Canada, to the United States. And this leads us to the question, "No, really, where are you from?" Michelle says that she's never been asked that—at least not quite in that way. Generally, she says, if someone asks where she's from, she tells them she's an Alberta girl—born and raised. If they want more specific information, she tells them she's from Calgary. And, more often than not, Michelle says, people are happy with that answer. Interestingly enough, however, she says that the ones who are most likely to dig further are people of colour.

"In that case," she says, "I pretty much know what they're asking, so I just say that my parents are from China, and I was born here in Canada."

In the end, Michelle is grateful for having been born in Canada and that she has been able to take advantage of all the opportunities that spun off of that. I ask Michelle what Calgary is like, from her perspective, when it comes to acceptance (or rejection) of the Chinese culture.

"I've been super lucky," she tells me, "I've worked for nine years for a boss who sees my culture as an asset. But there's a flip side to it, too. I once tried to get into a club, and they were barring people of colour. That was in the early 1990s. We ended up just boycotting it. We never went back. And today, if it's just one or two Chinese people entering a bar, it's fine. But if there are eight or ten, it does raise some eyebrows. It's stereotyping, yes, but it makes people nervous to think that it might be a gang."

Of course, Michelle points out, it's not just the Chinese who run into this, but other visible minorities as well. And sometimes it's as much about attire as it is about ethnicity. Michelle tells me that she's heard that an Asian wearing an "Affliction" T-shirt often isn't allowed entry into a club because "only drug dealers can afford that type of shirt."

But in her 15 years in Calgary, Michelle has seen more enclaves of visible minorities sticking together, forming communities, and finding ways to feel safer. For instance, the Filipino community is quite large in Calgary and forms pockets of communities. If you go to a particular neighbourhood, such as Southland, and go into the mall, you will see that about 90 percent of the clientele are white. But if you go into Marlborough Mall in the northeast, you will see the reverse, where the majority of clients are people of colour.

"It's like two different worlds," Michelle says. "If these groups do meet, it would probably be at an event such as the Calgary Stampede.

"I think," she adds, "that the white and non-white divide is still there."

"You don't see the gap closing?" I ask.

"No. I don't feel that," Michelle says. "I see people sticking to their own communities, not blending together as much as they could. I do see it in classrooms where a rich and diverse experience can exist. But when the students leave school, or when they go into the workforce, it doesn't appear to me to be very diverse at all. Even where I work, there are three people of colour, including me — everyone else is white."

Not only are Michelle's work colleagues predominantly Caucasian, but her friends are as well. She tells me that she has about one Chinese friend for every ten Caucasian friends. This, she points out, is a reflection of what she experienced growing up. The professionals in Michelle's life — her accountant, physician, dentist, etc. — aren't Chinese either. Michelle tells me that she decides those things on a person-by-person basis, not based on culture.

"It's kind of funny," she says. "I see how my mom will give up her parking space, but only for another Chinese person. She sees it as a tradition — an obligation to help out 'her own.' But I've never felt that way at all."

So, given that there are few other Chinese people in Michelle's social circle, what does she do to maintain her culture? At first glance, not a lot. She does celebrate Chinese New Year with a small group of Chinese friends, but doesn't participate in any other events throughout the year. And she does still speak some Chinese to her family, but her grasp of the language is basic at best.

"I've been asked to be on certain committees and boards and stuff," she says, "but when I go, I feel I'm not Chinese enough to be effective. I can't speak or read the language well enough to communicate, and I don't have ties to the community. I even felt this when I was in university. There were Chinese university groups, and I knew about them, but I wouldn't join them."

Although Michelle's mom still gives red envelopes (a monetary gift given in a red envelope during holidays or special occasions), prays to ancestors, and performs other traditional Chinese customs, Michelle just isn't in that same place.

"Do I feel close and all of that? No," Michelle says. "Do I want to? Yeah, sometimes I do."

Michelle tells me that she has a picture of herself with her grandparents and a roasted pig. The picture was taken in St. Paul during a Chinese New Year celebration when Michelle was very young.

"You know," she says, "I don't know if I know enough about what the Chinese cultural lifestyle really is to say I would never do it. And I don't know all of the Chinese phrases and lessons, like obey your parents and stuff like that, to really be able to tell to what extent I follow them."

Michelle does know, however, that if her mother ever needed Michelle to take care of her, Michelle would certainly do it. And when

Michelle's dad asked her for money, Michelle didn't so much as ask what he needed it for. These actions stem from parts of her that she feels are very Chinese — attitudes that are innate and unspoken.

And Michelle has discovered, and continues to discover, herself and her Chinese culture in less traditional ways. Her struggles with the push and pull between Chinese culture and mainstream culture can be seen clearly in her films. While Return Home, her first film, is mostly a "positive" movie that follows her family's journey and focuses on culture and understanding, her second film, Pieces of a Dream, tackles some more troubling areas, such as gambling addictions and suicide. The film is, once again, about Michelle's Chinese family, but it's also about the secrets the family has carried. Needless to say, the film wasn't very well received in the Chinese community, which frowns darkly on revealing secrets and airing one's dirty laundry in public.

Michelle tells me that when the film was first being promoted, the Chinese community felt that a film about suicide and gambling would bring shame to the Chinese community — and for a Chinese person, there is nothing worse than "losing face." Regardless of how irrational it may appear to an outsider, sharing personal experiences that might be seen as negative with the outside world is strictly taboo.

"It was like they were saying to me that I shouldn't ever bring any of this stuff up. Like, 'you're giving us a black eye, and we have enough of our own problems already without you adding to them.'"

Nevertheless, this is the road that Michelle has taken and will continue to take. It's a road that has helped her to sort out a lot of issues that have arisen because of both her culture and her sexuality. And Michelle tells me that she is definitely more proud of being a Chinese-Canadian now than she was when she was a child.

"Growing up, I didn't really even understand the Chinese part," she says. "And a 'Canadian' was a white person. But now I get that 'Canadian' includes a multicultural spectrum. And I'm a part of that."

Whether it's her culture or her sexuality, Michelle has bravely tackled the issues of life and has, for the most part, emerged victorious. She is a successful, independent, confident person who just happens to be female, Chinese, and a lesbian. That's just who she is. In essence, Michelle J. Wong has found herself.

We Are Family

One warm December morning, I hop onto a Greyhound bus and make my way from Edmonton to Calgary to interview Wayne Leong. During the entire interview with Wayne, I find myself in a bit of a state of disbelief. I can't believe I'm hearing stories about a close-knit Chinese family. I don't come from one, and most of the other people I interviewed don't come from one either. To be honest, I always thought that a close Chinese family was something that you just might… maybe… encounter on TV. Until now.

Wayne Leong was born in Taber, Alberta (famous for its "Taber corn"), and was raised in Vauxhall, a small Alberta town about a 20-minute drive from Taber and a two-hour drive from Calgary. Vauxhall is an oil, gas, and agricultural town, and at the time of our interview, Wayne tells me the population of Vauxhall is approximately 1,000. And there has been no increase in population since Wayne left in the 1980s.

Ming and Sue Leong, Wayne's parents, were both born in China. Ming was from YinPing and Sue from the Toishan area, both located in the southern part of China. Still, the couple didn't meet until after Sue came to Canada with the specific purpose of marrying Ming. The marriage between Sue and Ming was arranged by relatives. At the time, Sue was living in Hong Kong and became friendly with her downstairs neighbours, who had connections to both Ming's relatives and Sue's relatives. It was through this connection that members of both families ensured it was a suitable match and made arrangements for Sue to travel to Canada, where the couple would be wed.

Wayne's parents owned a restaurant in Vauxhall. It was originally called the Modern Café, but was renamed Ming's Restaurant after Wayne's father built an addition. Wayne's father had always worked in the restaurant business, and he owned and ran the restaurant in Vauxhall for 35 years before he moved to Calgary to be closer to his sons.

Wayne tells me that he learned a lot growing up working in the restaurant.

"I learned a strong work ethic, for sure. We started working really young. I was only five or six years old, and I had to sweep the floor before I went to school.

"It also made us stick together. It was a way of providing a living; it forced us to work hard, and it made sure we stayed focused on doing the best we could."

Wayne doesn't feel that the restaurant segregated him from his classmates at all—in fact, the restaurant was at the dead centre of Vauxhall, making it a natural meeting place. The school the children attended was four or five blocks from the restaurant, and the Leongs lived one block from the restaurant. So working in the restaurant provided lots of exposure to the public, including classmates. At the forefront of his job in the restaurant, was hospitality and providing guest services.

"My mom taught us to always be humble and to not be boisterous because we were relying on the people around us so that we could earn a living. It's important, in Chinese culture, to be humble in the public eye. And even though we were exposed to the public a lot, we were still quite reserved and tended to stick to ourselves as a family."

I ask Wayne what his parents' ideals were for raising the three boys.

"They wanted us to balance both cultures. At home, they insisted that we always speak Chinese (the Toishan dialect), and they wouldn't speak English to us. I'm not sure, but looking back at it, I think that might have had an effect on how well we did in school. But then again, maybe we were just lazy," Wayne laughs.

Wayne's parents also told the boys many stories about China and their experiences growing up there, and they passed on a never ending series of family anecdotes and wisdoms.

"But not only did they encourage us to understand the Chinese culture," Wayne says, "they also encouraged us to understand and absorb everything we were taught in school. They allowed us to go to church and Sunday school, even though neither of them was a Christian: my mom was Buddhist and Taoist, and my dad was Taoist. They really encouraged us to experiment with a lot of different things."

Wayne's parents did, however, expect the boys to achieve to their highest potentials no matter what they did.

"Because we're part of a minority, Chinese, the expectation from our parents," Wayne tells me, "was that we had to make damn sure we didn't just achieve, but overachieve. Because the Chinese were put down for the longest time for not conforming, it was like they expected an acceleration of our abilities."

"Because that's a way to gain respect?" I ask.

"Exactly," Wayne says. "You had to perform—you had to be the outstanding performer so that they can't keep kicking you down. If you just fit into the status quo, you won't survive. Being an overachiever was the only way out, and the only way to ensure respect. And that's why, to this day, our family's drive is unwavering. My parents demonstrated this idea day in and day out, and because of that, I truly believe it."

Though Wayne fit in quite well with his classmates at school, the older students from higher grades often gave him grief. This, Wayne believes, is because intolerance stems from ignorance. If you teach your classmates about your culture, he says, they will have a better understanding of both your culture and you as a person. Because these older students didn't have any Chinese classmates, they were much more ignorant of the culture, thus resulting in the discrimination faced by Wayne and his brothers.

"When we walked home from school," Wayne tells me, "people would definitely call us names and beat us up. This went on from about grades one to seven—when we were too young to fend for ourselves. At the time, we just dealt with it. When we walked home, we avoided certain routes. We would walk down back alleys just so that no one would see us. We would 'sneak' home."

In Vauxhall, there were both kids who lived in town and kids who lived on farms. The farms kids were always bussed back to their homes after school, so Wayne socialized more with the town kids, who were all Caucasians. Wayne reminds me that not all of the Caucasian kids in Vauxhall were bad. In fact, he had many Caucasian friends who would drop by the restaurant and just hang out with him. And it was Caucasian friends who invited the boys to attend Sunday school.

"I remember," Wayne recalls, "our mom getting our little suits ready for us and giving us each a quarter so that we could give it as offering at Sunday school."

Still, Wayne and his brothers attended Sunday school only a few times.

"After going a few times," Wayne says, "we started to get picked on. Not ever by the people who had invited us, but by other people who were there. And nobody ever said anything to correct it, so we just stopped going. I remember my mom asking us why we didn't go anymore and us telling her that we didn't like it. But the truth is that it's pretty hard to return to a place where you don't feel welcome. We might not have known the word 'discrimination' but even a kid can feel the tension of it."

Wayne's entire family also experienced racism in Vauxhall. But, before he goes on, he is adamant about making it clear that not all of the people in Vauxhall were like that—that there were actually many people who condemned racist behaviour. There was, Wayne says, just the odd incident instigated by people who didn't have an understanding of the Chinese culture. Episodes of "dine and dash" were one example; others include customers wrecking things in the restaurant, making fun of the Chinese language and the types of food the Leongs ate, mimicking the Chinese language in a derogatory manner, or throwing rocks at the restaurant.

There was, however, at least one incident that was more serious.

"I remember that when I was about six or seven, some guys wanted to beat up my dad. And it was so hard to sit and watch my father, who was just trying to earn a living, be confronted with things that just shouldn't happen in the normal course of doing business."

Wayne describes his father as a strong man who his three sons looked up to and learned a lot from. A man who taught his children that sometimes in life it's important to be humble, non confrontational, and patient, and to accept the way things are.

"Even then," Wayne says, "the one thing I gave my dad credit for was that, even when he was targeted by discrimination, he remained composed. He remained humble and forgiving. He would fight back for the safety of his family, but as far as his own 'self' went, he just took it—he would let it bounce off his shoulders, and he would continue on."

The only extended family the Leongs had in Vauxhall was Wayne's great uncle Johnny (who would ultimately live to be 103). Uncle Johnny was Wayne's grandfather's brother who had settled in Vauxhall quite some time before Wayne's family did. In fact, Uncle Johnny was the reason that Wayne's father ultimately chose Vauxhall as the place to open a restaurant and raise his family. Wayne grew up with his second cousins, Uncle Johnny's children, and they all got together for Christmas, New Years, and Chinese New Years. Similar to millions of Chinese people worldwide, roasted pigs and other traditional foods, red envelopes, and, of course, prayers to their ancestors were a part of the Leongs' celebrations.

Other than Uncle Johnny, no other family members, including Wayne's parents' siblings, ever immigrated to Alberta. Both Wayne's paternal and maternal grandparents, however, did immigrate to the United States.

There was one other non related Chinese family in Vauxhall when Wayne was growing up: the Hau family. The Hau family owned a farm close to Vauxhall. Because the Hau children (who were around the same age as Wayne and his brothers) were "farm kids" and Wayne was a "town kid," Wayne didn't hang out with them as much as he did with his Caucasian friends, but the two families did interact and socialize together. In fact, Wayne still keeps in touch with the Hau family today.

Not surprisingly, Wayne felt more comfortable with the Hau kids than he did with his other friends. The "fit" was just so much more comfortable both culturally and conversation wise. Whereas Wayne had so much in common with the Hau kids, when he was with his other friends—even when he wasn't facing discrimination—he was always aware that he was "different" because of the foods he ate and his own unique experiences as a Chinese person.

His interactions with the Hau kids as opposed to Caucasian kids really reinforced the differences and struggles between the two cultures. Still, he didn't ever really experience any personal, internal conflict or cultural struggles. His biggest struggle, he says, was trying to explain Chinese culture to his non Chinese friends in ways they could understand.

Overall, Wayne says, Vauxhall was a good place to grow up. But the town soon became too small for Wayne and his ambitions. In 1980, at the age of 18, Wayne left Vauxhall and moved to Calgary, where he attended SAIT (Southern Alberta Institute of Technology). There, he took the Hotel and Restaurant Business program, which he thoroughly enjoyed and ultimately gave him the knowledge and the inspiration he needed to open his own restaurant in Calgary.

Wayne doesn't think that being a restaurant owner has brought him any closer, or taken him any further from, his Chinese heritage. Work is work, he says, and is a separate thing from culture. You can choose any occupation you wish: in the end, it's the family values you grow up with that will determine which way you go, according to Wayne. I did notice, however, that the clientele at Wayne's family restaurant (the Melrose Café and Bar located on Calgary's infamous "Red Mile") is mostly Caucasian, and I wonder if his answer would be different if the restaurant catered more to a Chinese clientele. Of course, I have no way of knowing the answer to that.

I tell Wayne that I can see how much of the work ethic he learned from his parents has gone into the Melrose Café and Bar. From the outside, it looks like any nice restaurant in the trendy area of the city. But when you step inside, you almost want a tour of the place. It's truly impressive, with a huge beautiful patio divided by terraces providing privacy for customers. Then there's the theatre room, with two life-sized Terracotta Chinese Warriors standing on guard ready to protect you (not that there's anything to be afraid of!). A section of the restaurant features an enormous stone Buddha, and in another section, a huge Chinese coin is predominantly displayed on the wall. If you want something a little less formal, or you're feeling competitive, you can go play pool in the lounge. I've truly never seen anything else like it—a red lounge, a theatre, a bar, a restaurant, and an atrium all under one roof. Wayne's restaurant may not have had much influence on his Chinese perspectives, but it's pretty clear that Wayne has had a Chinese influence on the Melrose Café and Bar.

The restaurant is a reflection of what is important to Wayne and his family: their customers, the Chinese culture, and hard work. I tell

Wayne that I can see those high expectations that we've been talking about in the care that he's taken to create such a unique experience for his customers. And, although Wayne told me earlier that high expectations are a good thing, he admits to me now that there is a downside to them as well. It can, he says, create a huge internal struggle. He feels like he's always being put to the test—and failure is never an option. He must achieve and keep achieving…always.

I ask Wayne if, in his own restaurant, he still experiences the same types of episodes of racism that his family experienced back in Vauxhall. He tells me he doesn't—or at least not to that extent. Any racism he runs into now is very subtle. He believes that tolerance, in general, tends to be greater in large cities than it is in small towns. And then there is the factor of time, this being a different day and age than that in which Wayne grew up. In fact, when he tells people about his experiences in Vauxhall, many of them react with disbelief that such things could have happened.

I ask Wayne how he's involved with the Chinese culture today, now that he has moved away from Vauxhall and his childhood. He says he found the Chinese culture fascinating when he was a child, and he still does. Though he doesn't read or write Chinese, he can still speak it, though he doesn't always exercise that ability. For instance, Wayne's dentist is Chinese and speaks the language, but Wayne says that they never speak Chinese to one another. But there are many other ways, besides language, in which Wayne connects with his culture.

"I especially understand the cultural respect for our elders, including elders who have passed on, such as my grandfather. We respect our ancestors to such a great degree—I always found that fascinating as a child. As I was growing up, I would ask more and more questions about it, and I keep learning more. I've visited my grandfather's burial site in China at the insistence of my parents, and it was a really interesting experience. In our culture, there's a lot of vertical respect."

"What does 'vertical respect' mean?" I ask.

"Well, a really good example is the process that occurs during New Year's celebrations. When you go to your elders, you're supposed to wish them a happy New Year, and they, in turn, give you leisei (red envelope with money inside). That's what vertical respect is: you give them respect first, and they, in turn, give it back to you in the form of a leisei. It reinforces the respect in our culture and that's really important."

Wayne feels very fortunate to have this deep understanding of respect, something he feels that mainstream western culture is sadly lacking in.

Wayne also belongs to the Leong Society, which is, as one might guess, a "society" of Leong family members from Calgary and surrounding areas who gather for fundraising, social events, banquets, and celebrations.

Since Wayne has no children, nor is he married, I ask him about his nieces and nephews, who range from 1 to 21 years of age and in their involvement in Chinese activities. He tells me that none of them go to Chinese schools because they are already so active that there's simply no time for it, especially on the weekends. None of the kids speak Chinese fluently, but they do speak a bit and can understand it — at least enough to understand their grandparents. They do, however, respond to their grandparents in English.

Wayne says he can't speak on his brothers' behalves, but if he had to guess, he would say that their experiences with Chinese culture and identity are probably consistent with his. Besides being very close in age to one another and sharing very similar experiences, they also had very consistent upbringings because their parents always insisted on treating them all the same. This, Wayne adds, may well be another reason he never experienced a cultural identity crisis or tug of war when he was growing up.

No one in Wayne's immediate family has married a non Chinese person. One of his second cousins, however, did — which elicited a somewhat strong reaction from the entire family.

"We're always encouraged to only be involved in relationships with someone from our own culture," Wayne says. "In fact, it's pretty much insisted."

"Is it an unspoken insistence?" I ask.

"Oh no, it's spoken. It's clearly communicated and insisted upon. And that's one of the struggles of being brought up in a western society whereby we have to establish relationships and friendships with people who aren't Chinese because there's no other choice. It's difficult — there's an element of bias in the eyes of the family, for sure."

As briefly mentioned throughout the book, a Chinese marrying a non Chinese is often seen as a traitor, or an outcast. But there's a reason why marrying an outsider in the Chinese culture, is taboo. Wayne notes that's at least partially a result of the opinions that older Chinese people have formed because of the prejudice they themselves have been subjected to at the hands of mainstream culture. They hold very strong views about who they want their children to be involved with, and it's only natural that they would do so. They had to 'stick to their own kind,' as a result of being victimized by mainstream society.

As for Wayne and his brothers, their parents made it very clear to the boys that they are to date and marry only Chinese women. Wayne tells me that he and his brothers have always felt they would be risking great shame and endless family gossip should they marry someone who was not Chinese. For Wayne, this has been a cause of struggle.

"As it happens," he says, "my significant other is Chinese. But between being brought up in an environment where there were very few Chinese people that I wasn't related to and my parent's insistence that I could date only Chinese people, it was really difficult. I always had this internal struggle — this question of, 'Why does this have to be the case? If a person is a good person, why does it matter?' But I do understand that my parents faced a lot of discrimination, which resulted in them discriminating in turn. And it's not like we set ourselves apart — we were set apart by others. Because of the way we looked, or talked, or the food we ate. It's actually pretty easy to see why the older generation would associate Caucasian people with abuse."

And differing opinions within the Chinese community only added to the confusion for Wayne.

"Our parents told us we couldn't date non Chinese people, but we had non Chinese friends. And then there were others who weren't even receptive to friendships with non Chinese people. And then there were those who were completely receptive to the idea — so it was a bit confusing. How come some families welcome it and some don't?"

It is, however, a learning process for everyone, Wayne believes. And even his parents' attitudes have evolved in the last few years. As for Wayne, at the end of the day, he will choose what's best for him. He is older and wiser now, and can see the good and bad in both cultures, and he knows what to take from each and what to leave behind. And, he's glad that his parents, as they got older, embraced a similar attitude. He says that understanding both cultures gives him a sense of harmony.

Wayne continues to learn more about his Chinese heritage through the things that his parents taught him and his visits to China, of which there have been several. Because his parents were having a hard time running the restaurant and taking care of three boys at the same time, Wayne lived in Hong Kong with his grandmother for a brief period when he was young. But Wayne remembers little of that time in his life (he was about three when he left Canada, and five when he returned). However, his subsequent trips as a teenager and in the last few years have had a significant impact on him.

Each visit was very different than the one before because of the constant evolution of the country. I tell Wayne that I think he's extremely lucky to have experienced the Mao years, the pre-1997 years, and the post-1997 years. He is one of the few people, outside of those who actually live in China, to have witnessed the transformations China has experienced in those time frames.

Despite having witnessed China's often painful growing pains, Wayne is hungry for more.

"It's absolutely fascinating," he says. "I still want to go back and learn more about it. I want to learn about the different cities and the different parts of China. There's so much more to it than Guangdong province. We North Americans tend to think we're the centre of the universe. But when you go to China, you find out that they don't care about westerners. They have their own lives and their own world, and they believe that they're actually more advanced than us. And they probably are."

There are a lot of really wonderful things to see in China. Wayne tells of his trip to Xian, site of the Terracotta Warriors: hundreds and hundreds of warriors lined up ready for battle, ready to protect their emperor, housed in an area the size of a football field. This was an accidental, once-in-a-lifetime discovery by Chinese peasants who were digging a well for water and, instead of finding water, found this historic tomb.

With great excitement, Wayne tells me that there are a couple of similar tombs that archeologists don't even dare touch because of the build up of mercury vapors inside of them. It would be far too dangerous for anyone to inhale the fumes, and the introduction of oxygen to the site would cause the original colours of the warriors to disintegrate. So the tombs must remain sealed until someone can figure out how to prevent the negative chemical reaction that would result from a collision between mercury and oxygen.

Wayne found the Chinese Terracotta Warriors absolutely fascinating (hence the replicas in his restaurant), and he also felt the same historic energy at the Great Wall of China.

I can hear in Wayne's voice how exhilarating it is to him to be a part of this culture. But, he is equally proud to be Canadian. He feels fortunate to have been brought up in this country of opportunity and to have had the opportunity to go to China and learn about another side of himself.

"I'm proud of both," he says. "Proud to be Canadian and proud to have a Chinese heritage. A heritage I'm still learning about — still trying to understand what we're all about and how we've evolved."

I add that it's sometimes perplexing to look in the mirror and realize that you're looking at a face that has been 5,000 years in the making. Wayne agrees.

Wayne is also proud of the way that Canada as a whole has evolved—that the Chinese are largely accepted today and that there is no longer the lack of education that there used to be. He wouldn't trade his childhood experiences for anything because they are what shaped him into the person he is today. They, and his parents, have taught him about humility, enduring hardship, being patient, and persistence.

Wayne tells me that he has definitely been asked the question "where are you from?" often. But he doesn't mind—he sees it as a moment in which curiosity kicks in, and the time is ripe to open up a multitude of fascinating conversations about cultural identity and heritage. It is, Wayne says, a moment that leads to that thing which he has been emphasizing and promoting all along: education. And education, he says, makes all the difference.

Final Remarks

The composition of Canada's immigration began to see a qualitative change in the mid-20th century, which, in turn, changed the demographic landscape enormously. In the past 30 years, Canadian immigration policy has shifted dramatically, affecting the volume, characteristics, and admission of immigrants (Simmons & Keohane 1992:422). Today, the majority of Canada's immigrants come from Asia, the Middle East, Latin America, and the Caribbean, unlike the early periods of Canadian immigration history when the majority of immigrants were of European background. In 1971, 40.4% of immigrants were from Europe, compared to 22.4% from Asia (McVey & Kalbach 1995: 94). In 1991, however, only 20.8% of immigrants were from Europe, compared to 52% from Asia (McVey & Kalbach 1995:94).

In the contemporary era, a new type of migration— "transnational migration"—is forming in response to the changing global economy. According to Schiller, Basch, and Blanc, "transnational migration is the process by which immigrants forge and sustain simultaneous multi-stranded social relations that link together their societies of origin and settlement" (1995:48). Today, global capital has also reconfigured and restructured the world, affecting international migration and nation state building. The new and more sophisticated forms of capital have also provided the context for current day immigrants established in any of the first-world nations to "maintain or construct new transnational interconnections that differ in their intensity and significance from the home ties maintained by past migrations" (Schiller et al., 1995:52). Although home ties were maintained in previous migra-tions, they were different from the home

Final Remarks 187

ties maintained today due to the restructuring of the global economy over the 134 years since Confederation. Besides political and capital changes, violence, war, poverty, famine, and the promise of a safer life are also driving forces behind the changes in transnational connections and migrations.

Lloyd Wong writes, "as the world economy becomes more globally integrated and as Asian countries become more competitive in the world market, this type of migration (transnational migration) is gaining in importance" (1997:336).

Migration, of course, has a huge impact on the ethnic identities of both the migrants and their descendants. There are a number of definitions of "ethnic identity" in immigration literature, but they are more or less similar, and all of them emphasize the importance of common ancestry, shared cultural experience, and a positive commitment and devotion (socially and psychologically) to an ethnic group.

Monica Boyd writes, "...ethnic identity generally describes the psychological and social attachments of individuals to groups on the basis of shared ancestry and/or social and cultural attributes" (2000:139). Similarly, Leo Driedger describes ethnic identity as "a positive personal attitude and attachment to a group with whom the individual believes he [sic] has a common ancestry based on shared characteristics and shared sociocultural experiences" (Kalin & Berry 1985:3).

The issue of people's ability to maintain or lose that ethnic identity is the very heartbeat of this book. "Ethnic identity retention" is, simply put, "the extent to which attributes that can be identified as characteristic of a specific ethnic group are present among second or subsequent generations" (Isajiw 1990:34). In his significant 1990 article, Wsevolod Isajiw identifies five variables that indicate that an individual has maintained his or her ethnic identity. These five variables are as follows:

1) Having knowledge of, literacy of, and using the ethnic language;
2) Having ethnic in-group friendships;
3) Participating in ethnic group functions;
4) Having exposure to ethnic media, which keeps members in touch, provides an ethnic perspective on current events, and reinforces ethnic symbolism; and
5) Celebrating ethnic traditions such as participating in religious holidays, eating ethnic food, or appreciating ethnic artistic objects.

But ethnic identity is not only about the intensity of these ethnic ties. Fleras and Elliot (1999:119) write, "what is critical is the identification with select aspects of that cultural lifestyle—not the degree or intensity of that involvement." So, the immigrant may identify with only certain ethnic symbols, as opposed to sharing a common culture with his or her ancestral group. According to Isajiw, "assimilation into the culture of a larger society and retention of some forms of ethnic identity can and often do take place concomitantly (1990:35). In other words, the two identities—that of one's ethnicity and that of one's adopted culture are not mutually exclusive, but can indeed be complementary. Thus, it is possible both to have an ethnic identity and to participate fully in Canadian culture.

But as important as reading the literature on migration and ethnic identity is to understanding ethnic identity retention and/or loss, it is equally important to hear the stories of those who have first-hand experience of the issue. That is, to put a human face on the subject.

Initially, I thought that every story in this book would be somewhat similar, whereby everybody's families got along, there were minimal struggles, and there was a general acceptance of the Chinese culture.

Such was not the case. Although the theme of Chinese identity is prevalent throughout the book, the story of each interviewee is unique.

I was sometimes astonished by the honesty and openness of the people I talked to as they told me about their struggles with balancing Chinese and mainstream cultures and their not-so-perfect families. No one I talked to embraced the Chinese culture wholeheartedly right from beginning to end. And in every case, there were external conflicts, internal conflicts, family conflicts, and other kinds of conflicts. But these are true stories — sometimes they are messy and sometimes nothing like one would expect the "typical" Chinese story to be. When I say "typical", I meant a Chinese person who has never stepped outside of the Chinese box and had diligently and obediently followed the Chinese cultural rules to a 't'. I was wrong. What I found was that the degree and intensity of each of the interviewees stepping outside of that box, were different and yet unique to their situation and life history.

Another common thread throughout the book is, sadly, the presence of racism in all these people's lives. Racism was, and still is, an inevitable occurrence in the lives of members of visible minorities in Canada. If nothing else, I hope that this book will help all those people feel less alone — as it has for me.

There were several times while I was writing this book that I was shaken, rattled, and rolled. It would seem that every single person I talked to had something to teach me. Here are a few of the lessons I learned:

From Susan P., I learned that a parent's love (especially a Chinese parent's love) often comes through in ways that don't "fit" within the conventional North American ways of expressing love or saying "I love you." Thank you, Susan, for reminding me of this.

Kevin Kwan validated my repulsive feelings towards the shallow importance placed by the traditional (and maybe even the modern

Chinese way of thinking) Chinese culture, of pursuing a wealthy significant other. This topic wasn't part of his narrative, and it was just a little bit of information he mentioned that he doesn't agree on, but it made a huge impact on me. Thank you Kevin. I now know I'm not alone in feeling and thinking this way.

Marty Chan taught me that a Chinese marriage based on love, and not necessarily and predominantly on economic convenience, can happen in the Chinese culture. I was floored when he told me that his parents actually fell in love prior to marrying. Thank you Marty, for debunking the myth that marriages amongst the older Chinese generations were always based on economic and practical reasons — and never on love. And thank you for giving me back a bit of my idealism.

Mary Chan's story confirmed to me the incredible expectations and obligations placed on the eldest son of a Chinese family and the repercussions of that kind of pressure. This reminded me of my father and how I feel about him. And the whole idea of "spirit marriages" between the dead will be forever engraved in my mind. Thank you, Mary, for teaching me something new about my culture.

His Honour former Alberta Lieutenant Governor Norman Kwong and his wife Mary taught me that the sky truly is the limit, and, yes, even a Chinese person can make it to the "top," despite what history would tell us or what obstacles might get in our way. Thank you, Governor Kwong and Mary, for the inspiration.

Wei Wong inspired me to appreciate my ancestors more by never forgetting the sacrifices they made, and to never forget how resilient they were.

Michelle Wong taught me about courage. The courage to step right up to the batter's box and take a swing at fear. I might hit the ball, and I might miss it. If I miss, I miss. But if I hit it, boy, will it go far! Thank you, Michelle, for your example of bravery.

And, last but not least, from Wayne Leong, I learned that there is such a thing as a "close" Chinese family and building those kinds of families is something we, the younger generation, can aspire to. Thank you, Wayne, for giving me hope!

One of the many wonderful things to come out of the whole experience of writing this book is the friendships I have formed with the people I interviewed. I didn't think this would be an easy feat, but they made it easy by opening up their lives and sharing with me not only things related to being Chinese, but also perhaps things they had never revealed to anyone else before. They placed a trust in me that I will never forget, and I am deeply honoured to have been able to share their stories.

In their own special ways, the people in this book helped me draw out courage that I never knew I had. At first, I didn't think of this book as a vehicle for expressing myself. Rather, it was simply a means of telling the stories of others. But, in truth, it became a gift, an opportunity for me to speak more loudly.

Little did I know that when I finished my Master's degree twelve years ago, I would be given two gifts—a voice that I had suppressed for far too long and courage that was long overdue. I have truly been transformed by this experience.

I've always had a difficult time connecting with people—in fact, it used to be a paralyzing experience. But as I wrote this book, chapter by the chapter, the shackles came off. Initially, I didn't plan to write about myself at all, or so I thought. Until I interviewed these eight people, I didn't think I had a story at all. But writing their stories helped me find mine. And I hope this book will help others find theirs. Find it! And when you do, embrace all the rawness that comes with it.

Writing this book also forced me to get out of my old mindset. I had to constantly rethink and reword some of my questions to make it clearer and clearer. The questions may have been clear to me, but sometimes it was clear as mud for others. Also, I didn't realize how universal the concept of cultural/ethnic identity can be or how interchangeable it can be with other facets of our lives. Because of this journey, I now see the world a little differently. And I see myself differently. I had always hoped that this book might bring about change; little did I know that it would change me in profound ways that I could never have imagined.

It may seem like all of the stories in this book have positive outcomes, but it's important to remember that all of the interviewees had to go through painful periods in their lives to get to where they are today. Also, there is nothing saying that some of these people won't experience future struggles with their cultural identities. It would be extremely naïve of me to state that the retention and/or loss of ethnic identity is a black and white concept that never loses its shape.

I hope that No, Really, Where are you From? challenges readers in how they culturally categorize themselves and others. I purposely didn't categorize the chapters — or the people — in the book because I wanted the audience to understand that culture, ethnic identity, and racism affect everyone, regardless of background. This is our new world, and I want readers from all walks of life — not just the Chinese — to talk about it. While each of these stories is unique, the truth is that we are all much more alike than we are different. The road bumps through the peaks and valleys in the world of the Chinese culture (or any culture) are, in the end, pure human experiences. And, most importantly, it is those ethnic identity struggles (more for some than others) and conflicts between cultures that unite, rather than separate, us all.

Bibliography

Anderson, Kay J. Vancouver's Chinatown: Racial Discourses in Canada, 1875-1980. Montreal: McGill-Queen's University Press, 1991.

Beng, Tang Chee, Colin Storey, and Julia Zimmerman. Chinese Overseas Migration, Research and Documentation. Hong Kong: The Chinese University Press, 2007.

Breton, Raymond. "Institutional Completeness of Ethnic Communities and the Personal Relations of Immigrants." American Journal of Sociology 70 (1964): 193-205.

Boyd, Monica. "Ethnicity & Immigrant Offspring." Perspectives on Ethnicity in Canada. Eds. Madeline Kalbach & Warren Kalbach. Toronto: Harcourt Canada, 2000. 137-154.

Chow, Lily. Sojourners in the North. British Columbia, Canada: Caitlin Press, 1996.

Con, Harry, Ronald J. Con, Graham Johnson, and Edgar Wickberg. From China to Canada: A History of the Chinese Communities in Canada. Ed. William E. Willmott. Toronto: McClelland and Stewart Ltd, 1982.

Fleras, Augie and Jean Leonard Elliott. Unequal Relations: An Introduction to Race, Ethnic, and Aboriginal Dynamics in Canada. Third Edition. Scarborough, Ontario: Prentice Hall Allyn and Bacon Canada, 1999.

Gokalp, Altan. "Migrant's Children in Western Europe: Differential Socialization and Multicultural Problems". in Charles Stahl (ed.), International Migration Today, Volume 2: Emerging Issues. Australia: UNESCO, 1988. 125-137.

Goldstein, Jay and Alexander Segall. "Ethnic Intermarriage and Ethnic Identity." Continuity & Change in Marriage & Family. Ed. Jean Veevers. Toronto: Holt, Rinehart and Winston of Canada, Limited, 1991. 165-176.

Isajiw, Wsevolod W. "Ethnic Identity Retention." Ethnic Identity and Equality: Varieties of Experience in a Canadian City. Eds. Raymond Breton, Wsevolod W. Isajiw, Warren E. Kalbach, and Jeffrey G. Reitz. Toronto: University of Toronto Press, 1990. 34-91.

Kalbach, Madeline A. "Ethnicity & the Altar." Perspectives on Ethnicity in Canada. Eds. Madeline Kalbach and Warren Kalbach. Toronto: Harcourt Canada, 2000. 111-120.

Kalin, Rudolph and J.W. Berry. "Ethnic and Civic Self-Identity in Canada: Analyses of 1974 and 1991 National Surveys." Canadian Ethnic Studies 27.2 (1985): 1-15.

Mancho, Santiago. "Role of Associations as Regards Second Generation Migrants, Especially from the Point of View of Maintaining Cultural Links with the Country of Origin." International Migration 20.3-4 (1982): 85-101.

Maykovich, Minako K. "To Stay or Not to Stay: Dimensions of Ethnic Assimilation." International Migration Review 10.3 (1976): 377-387.

McVey, Wayne W. and Warren E. Kalbach. Canadian Population. Scarborough, Ontario: Nelson Canada, 1995.

Pan, Lynn. The Encyclopedia of the Chinese Overseas. Singapore: Archipelago Press, Landmark Books, 1998.

Pan, Lynn. The Encyclopedia of the Chinese Overseas. Cambridge, Massachusetts: Harvard University Press, 1999.

Richard, Madeline A. Ethnic Group and Marital Choices: Ethnic History and Marital Assimilation in Canada, 1871-1971. Vancouver: University of British Columbia Press, 1991.

Richmond, Anthony R. Post-War Immigrants in Canada. Toronto: University of Toronto Press, 1967.

Richmond, Anthony and Warren E. Kalbach. Factors in the Adjustment of Immigrants and their Descendants. Statistics Canada. Ottawa: Minister of Supply and Services, Canada, 1980.

Schiller, Glick Nina, Linda Basch, and Cristina Blanc. "From Immigrant to Transmigrant: Theorizing Transnational Migration." Anthropological Quarterly 68.1 (1995): 48-63.

Simmons, Alan B. and Kieran Keohane. "Canadian Immigration Policy: State Strategies and the Quest for Legitimacy." Canadian Review of Sociology and Anthropology 29.4 (1992): 421-452.

Sowell, Thomas. Migrations and Cultures: A World View. New York: Basic Books, 1996.

Takaki, Ronald T. A Different Mirror: A History of Multicultural America. Boston: Little, Brown & Co., 1993.

Ward, Margaret. The Family Dynamic: A Canadian Perspective. Second Edition. Scarborough: Nelson Canada, 1998.

Wong, Lloyd. "Globalization and Transnational Migration: A Study of Recent Chinese Capitalist Migration from the Asian Pacific to Canada." International Sociology 12.3 (1997): 329-351.

Yee, Paul. Struggle and Hope: The Story of Chinese Canadians. Toronto: Umbrella Press, 1996.

Appendix

These are the questions that guided my interviews, which pertained to a Chinese individual born and raised in a small Canadian town:

1. Tell me as much as possible about the town you were born and raised in. How old were you when you left there, and where did you go after that? Would you want to go back there to live again?

2. In the town you grew up in, did your parents work in occupations that were part of mainstream culture (i.e. professionals) or did they own their own business? How did this make you feel in terms of how it has shaped you as a Chinese person or a Canadian person? In other words, besides the important fact that it has provided you food, shelter, clothing, and all the necessities of life, do you think your parent's occupation played an important role in how you saw yourself when you were growing up?

3. Where were your parents born? What were their ideals for raising you and your siblings? Did your parents encourage you to maintain your Chinese culture or was it more important to them that you fit into mainstream society?

4. Did you maintain your cultural language as you were growing up? How about now?

5. Did you have a presence of extended family when you were young? If so, were they involved in the Chinese culture?

6. Has anyone in your family married a non-Chinese person? If so, what was the reaction of your family or extended family?

7. As a member of a minority, did you feel like you fit in in the town you lived in and/or the school you attended? Did you have a lot of Caucasian/other visible minority friends?

8. Were there other families of the same cultural background as you in the town you lived in? If so, how many? Did you feel more or less comfortable around them? Did you hang around more with the kids of the same cultural background (if there were any) or did you feel more comfortable around Caucasians/other visible minority? If there weren't other Chinese children, what were the cultural backgrounds of your friends when you were young? Now?

9. Do your siblings share the same views as you on the Chinese culture/mainstream culture? How were their experiences the same or different from yours?

10. As you were growing up, did you experience a cultural identity crisis or feel a tug of war between the two cultures? Now?

11. Did you or your family experience subtle or direct racism when you were growing up? What about now? How do you feel about it and have those feelings changed or stayed the same as you grew older?

12. Do you feel there is more or less tolerance for your cultural background in large cities as compared to small towns?

13. What activities related to your cultural background are you involved in now? Examples: reading the Chinese paper, Chinese New Year celebrations, Chinese choirs, Chinese associations, etc. If you have kids, do/did they go to Chinese language schools? What language do you speak at home? Do you encourage your children/family to be involved in the Chinese culture? How?

14. Do you identify with some, none, or all of the Chinese cultural lifestyle?

15. Have you been to China? If so, what do you think of it? If not, do you have any interest in going there?

16. Is your physician, accountant, or dentist, etc. Chinese? Caucasian? Other? If they are Chinese, are their businesses located in Chinatown?

17. Do you think your cultural background has influenced, or will influence, your choice of a significant other?

18. Do you think your educational status or occupational status play a role in your cultural/ethnic identity retention or loss?

19. Are you more proud to be Chinese, Canadian, or both? Has your outlook changed or stayed the same from when you were growing up to now?

20. No, Really, Where Are You From? This question will be the title of my book. Have you been asked this question? If so, what are your thoughts when people ask you this question? If not, what do you think of this question?

* The second set of questions pertained to a Chinese individual born in the early 1900s. Only the first question is different, and the rest of the questions are the same as the first profile questions.

1. Tell me as much as possible about the city you were born in during your formative years (in the 1930s, 1940s, or 1950s). What was the cultural make-up in the city, during that time? What was happening to the city during those years?

Manufactured by Amazon.ca
Bolton, ON